# First Steps toward Reading

**By the Editors of Time-Life Books**

**Alexandria, Virginia**

TIME®
LIFE
BOOKS

Time-Life Books Inc.
is a wholly owned subsidiary of

# Time Incorporated

FOUNDER: Henry R. Luce 1898-1967

*Editor-in-Chief:* Henry Anatole Grunwald
*Chairman and Chief Executive Officer:*
J. Richard Munro
*President and Chief Operating Officer:*
N. J. Nicholas, Jr.
*Chairman of the Executive Committee:*
Ralph P. Davidson
*Corporate Editor:* Ray Cave
*Executive Vice President, Books:* Kelso F. Sutton
*Vice President, Books:* George Artandi

## Time-Life Books Inc.

EDITOR: George Constable
*Executive Editor:* Ellen Phillips
*Director of Design:* Louis Klein
*Director of Editorial Resources:* Phyllis K. Wise
*Editorial Board:* Russell B. Adams, Jr., Dale M.
Brown, Roberta Conlan, Thomas H. Flaherty,
Lee Hassig, Donia Ann Steele, Rosalind Stubenberg,
Kit van Tulleken, Henry Woodhead
*Director of Photography and Research:*
John Conrad Weiser

PRESIDENT: Christopher T. Linen
*Chief Operating Officer:* John M. Fahey, Jr.
*Senior Vice President:* James L. Mercer
*Vice Presidents:* Stephen L. Bair, Ralph J. Cuomo,
Neal Goff, Stephen L. Goldstein, Juanita T. James,
Hallett Johnson III, Carol Kaplan, Susan J. Maruyama,
Robert H. Smith, Paul R. Stewart, Joseph J. Ward
*Director of Production Services:*
Robert J. Passantino

Library of Congress Cataloging in
Publication Data
First steps toward reading.
  (Successful parenting)
  Bibliography: p.
  Includes index.
  1. Children — Books and reading. 2. Reading —
Parent participation. I. Time-Life Books. II. Series.
Z1037.A1F57 1987      649'.58      87-7067
ISBN 0-8094-5958-2
ISBN 0-8094-5959-0 (lib. bdg.)

## Successful Parenting

SERIES DIRECTOR: Dale M. Brown
*Series Administrator:* Norma E. Shaw
Editorial Staff for *First Steps toward Reading:*
*Designer:* Cynthia Richardson
*Picture Editor:* Jane Jordan
*Text Editors:* Robert A. Doyle, John Newton
*Staff Writer:* Margery A. duMond
*Researchers:* Rita Thievon Mullin (principal),
Mark Moss, Myrna Traylor-Herndon
*Assistant Designer:* Susan M. Gibas
*Copy Coordinators:* Marfé Ferguson,
Ruth Baja Williams
*Picture Coordinator:* Linda Yates
*Editorial Assistant:* Jenester C. Lewis

*Special Contributors:* Laura Akgulian, Megan
Barnett, Jaime Butler, George Daniels, Debbie Haer,
Angela Haines, William Miller, Wendy Murphy,
Barbara Palmer, Charles C. Smith (text); Barbara
Cohn (research)

Editorial Operations
*Copy Chief:* Diane Ullius
*Production:* Celia Beattie
*Library:* Louise D. Forstall

Correspondents: Elisabeth Kraemer-Singh (Bonn);
Maria Vincenza Aloisi (Paris); Ann Natanson
(Rome).

First printing. Printed in U.S.A.

Published simultaneously in Canada.
School and library distribution by
Silver Burdett Company, Morristown,
New Jersey 07960.

TIME-LIFE is a trademark of Time
Incorporated U.S.A.

*Other Publications:*

MYSTERIES OF THE UNKNOWN
TIME FRAME
FIX IT YOURSELF
FITNESS, HEALTH & NUTRITION
HEALTHY HOME COOKING
UNDERSTANDING COMPUTERS
LIBRARY OF NATIONS
THE ENCHANTED WORLD
THE KODAK LIBRARY OF CREATIVE PHOTOGRAPHY
GREAT MEALS IN MINUTES
THE CIVIL WAR
PLANET EARTH
COLLECTOR'S LIBRARY OF THE CIVIL WAR
THE EPIC OF FLIGHT
THE GOOD COOK
WORLD WAR II
HOME REPAIR AND IMPROVEMENT
THE OLD WEST

*For information on and a full description
of any of the Time-Life Books series listed
above, please write:*
Reader Information
Time-Life Customer Service
P.O. Box C-32068
Richmond, Virginia 23261-2068
or call: 1-800-621-7026

This volume is one of a series about raising children.

# The Consultants

## General Consultant

**Dr. Judith A. Schickedanz,** an authority on the education of pre-school children and the preparation of preschool teachers, is an associate professor in the department of Early Childhood Education and head of the Early Childhood Learning Laboratory, both at the Boston University School of Education. Her published work includes *More Than the ABC's: Early Stages of Reading and Writing Development,* and the textbooks *Strategies for Teaching Young Children* and *Toward Understanding Children,* as well as many scholarly papers. Dr. Schickedanz is the author of the teacher-training filmstrip *Literacy Development in the Preschool,* and serves on the Early Childhood Committee of the International Reading Association. She has been a consultant to the Children's Television Workshop, producers of *Sesame Street.*

## Special Consultants

**Dr. Bruno Bettelheim,** who gives his expert view on the importance of traditional fairy tales on page 102, is Distinguished Professor of Education Emeritus and Professor Emeritus of both psychology and psychiatry at the University of Chicago. Born in Vienna in 1903, he received his doctorate from the University of Vienna; he came to the United States in 1939. Today Dr. Bettleheim is esteemed throughout the world as one of the greatest authorities on child psychology. Among his many celebrated books, the best known is *The Uses of Enchantment.*

**Dr. Patricia J. Cianciolo,** an internationally recognized authority on children's literature, advised on the essay on children's book illustrators *(pages 107-111).* A professor of Teacher Education at Michigan State University, Dr. Cianciolo is the author of *Illustrations in Children's Books* and *Picture Books for Children.* She is chairperson of the Children's Book Awards Committee of the International Reading Association, and has chaired the Newbery-Caldecott Awards Committee of the American Library Association.

**Dr. Bernice E. Cullinan,** an expert on children's literature, advised on the sections on how parents can encourage children's interest in reading and writing, *(pages 56-85)* and on storytime *(pages 90-117).* Dr. Cullinan is a professor of Early Childhood and Elementary Education at New York University and a past president of the International Reading Association. The author of *Literature and the Child* and editor of *Children's Literature in the Reading Program,* she has served on the Caldecott Award Selection Committee of the American Library Association, and is on the Coordinating Council of the National Reading Initiative, a nationwide program to promote literacy.

**Dr. David Elkind,** who expresses his opinion on the dangers of formal instruction for preschoolers on page 76, is Professor of Child Study and Resident Scholar at the Lincoln Filene Center of Citizenship and Public Affairs at Tufts University. The author of stories for children as well as research articles, Dr. Elkind is president of the National Association for the Education of Young Children. Dr. Elkind sounded the alarm against the high-pressure teaching of young children in his book, *The Hurried Child: Growing Up Too Fast, Too Soon.* In addition, he has written *All Grown Up and No Place to Go* and *Miseducation: Preschoolers at Risk.*

**Dr. Elfrieda H. Hiebert,** an educational psychologist, advised on the section devoted to formal instruction in schools *(pages 118-137).* Dr. Hiebert, an associate professor at the University of Colorado, is the author of many scholarly papers on children's early experiences with literacy. She collaborated on *Becoming a Nation of Readers: The Report of the Commission on Reading.* She serves as a consultant for Silver Burdett Ginn's reading program as well as for several state departments of education.

**Dr. Frank R. Vellutino** contributed the expert's box on dyslexia *(page 30).* A specialist on reading disorders, Dr. Vellutino is a professor in the Department of Educational Psychology and Statistics, as well as the director of the Child Research and Study Center, at The University at Albany, State University of New York. For twenty years he has conducted and evaluated research on normal reading and reading disorders; he is the author of *Dyslexia: Theory and Research,* as well as numerous scholarly articles. He is on the editorial boards of the *Journal of Educational Psychology* and the *Journal of Learning Disabilities.*

# Contents

# 1

# The Lure of Reading

Unlikely as it may seem, the joyful nine-month-old in the photograph opposite is already taking a first step toward learning to read. Although he may not yet know that a book contains words and that the words convey messages, he has discovered that it is something to hold, fondle, and explore. Before long, he will be pointing excitedly to the pictures and naming the objects they represent as his mother or father reads to him. By the time he is three, he will enjoy hearing stories over and over. By four or five, he will have memorized some of his favorite storybooks and want to "read" them to his parents or younger siblings. By the age of six, when he enters elementary school and receives his first formal instruction in reading, he will be well on his way to becoming a lifelong reader.

Learning to read is a complex process that begins almost at birth. The impulse to learn flows naturally from a child's curiosity about the world around him and from his desire to gain mastery over himself and his environment. The learning is fed by his steadily growing understanding of language and his interest in the magical power of words.

As with other aspects of early childhood, the development of literacy involves a series of predictable milestones. But because children have their own internal timetables, based on their individual personalities and experiences, they reach these milestones at different points in their lives. Your goal should not be to push your child toward proficiency, but to help him get there at his own pace and in his own way. In fulfilling this goal, you will be helping to foster in him an abiding appreciation of reading, not only as the key to learning, but as one of life's most relaxing and pleasurable pastimes.

# Reading's Surprisingly Early Beginnings

Most parents think of learning to read as a process that starts in kindergarten or first grade. But reading and writing begin long before formal schooling, as children come face to face with written language in the world around them. It is tied closely to oral language skills, which develop at about the same time as emerging reading and writing skills and support them. In turn, the earliest experiences of young children with reading and writing reinforce each other in the development of literacy.

Your child learns to read and write for the same reasons that he learns to speak. As your child strives to understand his environment, he grows increasingly aware of the value of communication. If he is fully to connect with you and all those others who matter in his life, he must become literate. You can help him by creating the kind of atmosphere that will predispose him to reading and writing. Indeed, there is nothing greater you can do: Studies show that how much a youngster was read to in his early years most influences his reading proficiency in later years.

**Working out the puzzle** By definition, reading is the process of deriving meaning from printed words. Preschoolers who are just beginning to under-

stand the reading process use context — largely the illustrations in books — to predict content. But older children learning how to read realize that context alone is not enough and focus their attention on decoding, breaking the written words down into component sounds, and combining these into spoken words. The term *decoding* itself suggests how difficult — almost impossible — the process must be for a young child who barely knows the alphabet.

Children who have long been familiar with print in its many forms struggle relatively briefly with its mysteries before becoming fluent readers. As they progress, they combine their decoding skill with their knowledge of context to predict the meaning of whole words and phrases without having to laboriously sound them out.

Fluent reading, then, requires the young reader's mind to participate far more actively in the process than simply acting as the code-breaker for the images of letters rushing in through the eyes. Were his mind forced to register each letter, sound it out, and combine it with nearby letters until a familiar word could be recognized, reading for meaning would be nearly impossible for him. By the time he reached the end of the sentence, the beginning of it might be lost in the lengthy process of it all and be now only a dim memory.

Instead, he uses his knowledge of how language works and his experience with the topic of the piece being read to predict what will come next. He may, for example, confront the sentence, "A cat climbed up the tree." If he has never seen the word *climbed* written out before, he knows by its placement in the sentence that it is the action word. Further, from his experience with cats and trees, he knows that cats frequently go up them. Already he has narrowed the possibilities as to what the word might be. Seeing that it begins with *cl* will probably be enough for him to guess its identity correctly.

This ability to recognize that sentences typically are made up of subjects followed by verbs and objects becomes critical to his progress. He uses it to limit his possible choices as he confronts each new word. His knowledge of the subject at hand further restricts his choices, so that a quick glance at the first letters of a word may well be enough for him to know what it is and move along to the next one. Anyone who has ever faced a book written for specialists in a field about which he knows little, or who has tried to read an article in a foreign language in which his knowledge of grammar is shaky, can understand how important these tools are for fluent reading.

**Foundations of fluency**

During the preschool years children lay the base for fluent reading, learning about the world in general and about the way written language works. Long before he can begin to figure out which graphic symbols stand for what sounds, your child gradually becomes familiar with the conventions of print. He learns at least that books in this culture are read from left to right, and from top to bottom. And he learns that words are composed of a varying number of letters, are arranged in certain combinations, and have spaces on either side of them.

His constant discovery of information about the world is essential to his growing understanding of print conventions. Without such a frame of reference, he would be unable to correct himself when he makes a mistake reading or to figure out a word he has never seen before. Suppose, for example, that he encounters these sentences: "Mary went to look at her friend's house. The house had a red roof." If he mistakes *house* for *horse* in the first sentence, which is easy for a beginning reader to do, he will realize from the context of the next sentence that something is wrong and try again. A youngster who does not know what a horse is will not consider it necessary to revise his reading of the text, despite the incongruity. Rich background knowledge and the ability to use it to test the sense of the text are essential to reading competency.

Reading, like speaking, depends to a large extent on the informal instruction you provide your youngster during the preschool years, but this generally is so subtly given and received as to go almost unnoticed by parent and child alike. The formal instruction given in elementary school presumes that a child already is steeped in language. The youngster who lacks such enrichment usually lacks understanding of the reading process and thus has the most difficulty learning to read.

Children are sponges, absorbing an enormous amount of material before they ever enter school. Studies have shown that the average six-year-old has a vocabulary of more than 12,000

*A curious girl pauses to examine street markings, wondering what they mean. From explorations such as this, she develops print awareness — an emerging understanding of the importance of written language.*

words. She may not use them all, but they lie there in her brain, ready to tumble forth on command. In six short years she has learned to express herself and to ask the kinds of questions that continually broaden her knowledge. Her intuitive grasp of the rules of language is almost identical to that of a grownup. Incredible as these accomplishments may seem, they appear even more so when you take a moment to consider that they all occurred before your child has received any instruction in a classroom.

The analogy has been made that a little child learning her native tongue is like a young apprentice learning the trade of plumbing or carpentry. By observing and modeling herself on those around her, this young wordsmith eventually becomes skilled in the craft of speech. As in any apprenticeship, firsthand experience and trial and error are essential to the process. She makes assumptions about how language works, learning, for example, that verbs are changed into the past tense by adding *ed*. Incorporating this knowledge into her parlance, she makes errors, such as, "I runned all the way home." But these disappear over time as she not only masters and internalizes the rules of grammar but realizes that there are many exceptions to them.

**The meaning of experience**

Your youngster's awareness of words in printed form comes not only from her observations of you reading and writing but also from her awareness of the words everywhere around her — from the cereal box she sees first thing in the morning to the good-night story you read to her at bedtime. This, coupled with her natural curiosity, makes it possible for her to display an impressive familiarity with the written word at an early age. It is not long before she understands that print conveys messages, and soon she is actively engaged in attempting to figure out what those messages are.

Eager though many parents may be for their children to become proficient readers, they should not push them or lose patience with them. They sometimes fail to realize that their young ones have already made amazing progress toward literacy. A child who picks up a book, turns it right side up to look at the pictures, starts at the beginning, and scans the left page before the right one already knows a great deal about how print works. And if she scribbles horizontally on a piece of paper and asks her parent what she has written, she already understands a lot about writing. Such efforts should not be taken as an indication of how far she has to go toward becoming literate, but of how far she has already come. ⁛

# The Subtle Process of Language Development

The importance of your child's oral language development to his later reading proficiency cannot be overemphasized. In order to read, he must have not only a good vocabulary and a clear sense of the way language works, but he must also have an ear for the sounds, rhythms, and cadences of his native tongue. Motivated by a desire to fulfill his basic needs and to share his feelings with you and others, he acquires his language skills by listening to those around him and responding to them. Still, this is not enough. Here you enter the picture. In ways you may not even be aware of, you help pave the way for his becoming a reader.

**Communicating with love**

Infants have keen hearing from the day they are born. When a door accidentally bangs shut, they react by startling. When they hear soothing music, they calm down and go to sleep. But of all the sounds in their environment, the one they respond to most is the human voice, especially that of their mother.

Studies have consistently shown a relationship between a mother's responsiveness to her child and the child's later language competence. The affectionate exchanges between a mother and baby in the early weeks of life not only provide the child's first lesson in the importance of language as a social tool; they also contribute to the emotional security he needs to begin exploring his environment. A baby who is deprived of this close contact will begin to lag in language development when he is only six months old.

A mother communicates with a newborn and stimulates him in many ways. She may combine touch and sound, as when she traces a finger over the baby's face and labels the parts: "Eyes, ears, nose, and mouth." Or she may tickle his toes while reciting, "This little piggy went to market . . ." Long before the baby can understand what is being said to him, the pure pleasure of the situation makes him eager to respond. Invariably he does so by cooing when his mother stops speaking, learning through these conversations valuable lessons about turn-taking, as well as the joy that such communication can bring.

Whether vocalizing or merely listening, babies discover what sounds are important in language. By six months or so, they are capable of producing sounds appropriate to any language. Significantly, at about this age, they begin deleting from their repertoire any sounds not heard in the language spoken around them.

**Communicating without speech**

During her first few months of life, your child has the ability to make her needs known through a full range of expression. She cries when she is hungry, angry, or otherwise uncomfortable.

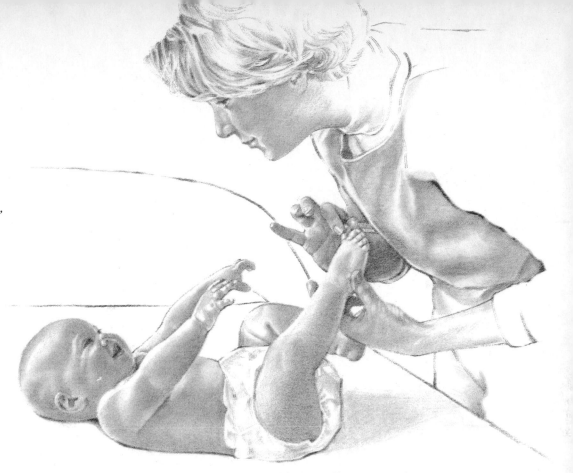

*Plainly delighted by "This little piggy went to market," a baby reaches out her arms toward her mother. Such parent-child interactions help teach the social aspects of language.*

When she is happy, she smiles, coos, and gurgles, and fixes you with a gaze of unmistakable contentment. When she is excited, she wiggles her whole body to tell you so.

Toward the end of her first year, your child will have found additional ways to get many of her intentions across through gestures and body language. She may clap her hands to tell you she wants to play pat-a-cake, wave bye-bye to someone who is leaving, and stretch out her arms to indicate that she wants you to pick her up.

At this same age she will probably relish experimenting with the sounds she can make. You may have noticed how, instead of crying immediately for attention when she wakens from her nap, she entertains herself in her crib with her babbling. Over and over, she repeats various sounds. Then she combines them with others and rehearses them some more, saying, "babababababa, dadadadada, badabadaba," in a voice that grows louder, then softer.

As her skill at vocalizing and her understanding of what you are saying to her increase, her exchanges with you become more sophisticated. Her babble increasingly takes on the intonations and cadences of adult speech. You will need to listen carefully to her: It will become quite apparent that she is expressing thoughts and feelings or simply making small talk. Although she has yet to utter her first words, her babbling has already become an important tool for communicating with you and others.

**Building to words**

Around the age of one, children generally add words to their repertoire of sounds and body language. Your child, who previously only pointed to a cupboard and squealed when she wanted something to eat may now point and say, "koo, koo," for "cookie." These one-word utterances usually stand for the names of familiar objects in her environment or express needs or responses, such as "drink" or "no." Still limited in vocabulary, she may use them to get across a variety of meanings. When she says "ball," she could mean "I see my ball," "I want to play ball," or "Where is my ball?" It is up to you to interpret her meaning.

At this stage of language development, most children enjoy repeating words after their parents. They may also begin pointing to an object and saying, "Dat" — often an indication that they want the parent to name the object for them.

By two, when they start using two- and three-word sentences, their speech begins to conform to simple rules of grammar and syntax. The little girl who says, "Doggie lick me," shows that she understands words have to be used in a certain order to make sense. By three, she has begun adding words and endings to words for more precise meaning. Her "Doggie lick me" has become "Betsy's doggie licked me." But while growing ever more proficient at language, she still makes mistakes. For instance, she may rearrange a word, saying "pasghetti" for spaghetti. Or she may exchange a word she knows with another one that sounds similar. A youngster fascinated with space and high technology might admire her father shaving with his "laser" blade.

*A game of monkey-see, monkey-do enables the happy child seen here to expand her growing repertoire of sounds. Even when she is alone, she will continue to practice by repeating the sounds over and over.*

Motivated by love for their children, most parents automatically provide the interaction and rich environment their youngsters need for language development. Mothers instinctively talk differently to a baby than they do to older children or to grownups, speaking more slowly and providing more pauses than would be true of adult speech. They use many more nonsense syllables, repetitions, variations in tone and pitch, and exaggerated facial expressions. They also

tend to simulate a two-way conversation, often asking questions that they answer themselves, until their children are old enough to participate fully in a dialogue.

As children grow older, this baby talk — or "motherese," as some linguists call it — gives way to more grown-up language. Sentences become longer and somewhat more complex. Once their children's vocabulary starts to expand rapidly, parents begin introducing new words, substituting *stomach* for *tummy,* for example, and in response to their youngsters' seemingly endless requests, they begin supplying the names of things.

Between the ages of two and three, many youngsters have come to feel so confident as speakers that their parents often find it difficult to get them to stop talking. In fact, some linguists believe that the "why" questions so characteristic of this period arise not only out of the youngsters' curiosity about the world but from a desire to keep the conversation going. They chatter on, not only asking questions but recalling things that happened to them. "I falled down and got a boo-boo on my finger," a child may eagerly tell a neighbor while holding out her hand to show off the wound that has long since healed. This ability to talk about events and objects that are remote or abstract represents a major step forward in language acquisition and yet another step toward reading. ✥

# A Head Start with Books

Just as they differ in temperament, all young children differ in the way they react to books. Some are happy to sit quietly while you read to them. Others who wiggle and squirm may be just as eager for a story to be read to them but will listen only if they can stay in constant motion. While you should keep in mind your child's age, interests, and personality when introducing him to books, you need not worry about starting too early. Studies have shown that even colorful pictures placed inside the crib of a newborn can capture his attention for a time, actually increasing his heartbeat. The important thing is to expose your youngster as often as possible to books to instill in him a love of reading and provide the background so essential to his later development as a reader.

**Enjoying books with babies**     Naturally, your young infant will not understand what you read to him. But he will delight in the warmth of being held in your arms and in your voice, so concentrated now and full of feeling. By the age of two or three months, most babies, when lying on their stomachs, can raise their heads by themselves long enough to focus on a bright, patterned picture of sharply contrasting colors. They may not know what the picture represents, but it will hold their attention for several moments; so, too, will nursery rhymes, with their compelling sing-song rhythms.

By six months, many children have become interested in books but would rather explore them with all their senses than listen to them being read. At this age your youngster may grab a book away from you and begin chewing or tearing it, oblivious to the fact that he is destroying it in the process. Nonetheless, as he grows accustomed to books through repeated exposure, his destructiveness will diminish while his ability to listen will gradually increase. By eight to ten months, he may even bring you a book, indicating that he wants you to read it for him. During storytime or when given the opportunity to explore books on his own, he will be more likely to look at the pictures than chew on the pages.

Between ten and fourteen months, most children are learning to walk, and they often find it difficult to sit still through an entire story. Yet their appreciation of books will have grown by leaps and bounds. When your child sees a picture he thinks is funny, he will laugh — a sure sign that his interest has been captured. By fourteen months, he may also begin jabbering as you read to him, almost as though he were trying to take over from you. This nonsensical chatter is called book babble because its tone is more formal than conversational. It indicates that your youngster has begun to realize that there is indeed a difference between the way written and spoken language sound.

Between fourteen and eighteen months, your child's speech is blossoming, and books can become an important source of amusement for him. Many children adopt a favorite storybook during this phase or become fascinated with a particular page, which they enjoy going back to over and over. Keep in mind that youngsters this age often express themselves in physical activity. A child who hears a story in which a youngster is scolded may remember his own anger at being scolded and jump up and down or yell. The book plainly has triggered a personal response. But without the skills to verbalize his feelings, he can react only physically.

Between the ages of nineteen and thirty months, your toddler's language skills take a giant stride forward. He begins speaking in sentences, and you can expect him to interrupt you frequently with his questions or his comments about the story while you are reading it aloud to him. He not only enjoys picking out the books for you to read, but he is likely to have memorized some of them and will be disturbed if you attempt to skip over words or pages or if you improvise a new variation on the story. He also comes to realize that reading

*A big brother does all he can do to keep a picture pamphlet out of harm's way. He knows that babies "read" books as they do all objects they wish to explore — by banging, chewing, and tearing them.*

17

is an effective way to postpone bedtime and often begs for "just one more story."

**Finding out how books work**

By the time they are two, many children have already been exposed to dozens of storybooks and have some idea of how books work. A child between the ages of eleven and fifteen months can tell when a book is upside down and will right it. Many two-year-olds know how to turn the pages correctly — that is, from front to back.

Still, most two-year-olds do not yet understand that the text of a book remains the same from one reading to the next. Ironically, this belief may be reinforced by their experiences of being read to aloud. Most parents wisely do not limit themselves to the text during storytime. Instead, they pause often, to relate objects or incidents to the child's own life and to ask or answer her questions. Such interaction encourages literacy development. Yet it also furthers the young child's notion that reading is linked somehow to the pictures.

Most three-year-olds continue to believe that pictures rather than the words of text tell the story. When they hold a book, they may obscure part of the print with their hands, failing to realize its importance. Or they may eagerly try to turn the page to get to a favorite illustration before you have finished reading all the words. Some, however, begin to show an awareness of the meaning of print. They may point to a label under a picture as you read it, indicating that they know the word is associated with the picture. Yet they will continue to use illustrations to interpret stories. Putting her finger on the word *rabbit,* for instance, a youngster may read it as *bunny.* But in doing so, she is nevertheless offering proof that she understands that spoken words have written counterparts. It remains now for her to learn the secret for figuring out which word is the right one.

At the same time, she is beginning to acquire familiarity with the vocabulary of reading. She comes to understand such words as *letter, word,* and *sound,* for example, through hearing them used by her parents. Her comprehension is further sharpened by questions. "What letter is that, sweetheart? Is that an *M?"* Or "What do you think those words say on the storybook?" Recognizing that a word starts with the same letter as her name, she might be told that both begin with the same sound.

**Immersed in print**

Clearly, once your child reaches the preschool years, she has a long way still to go before she becomes an actual reader. But

because you have read to her and encouraged her experiments with words, she will be motivated to imitate book-reading behavior earlier than children who have not had such support. And this, in turn, will have direct bearing on her reading experience in school. She may, for example, pretend to read to an audience of stuffed animals and do so with all the concentration you give to her while you are enjoying each other's company during a bedtime story.

This mimicking of adult book-reading leads to your youngster's independent explorations of print. A sure sign that your child is entering this phase of literacy development is when she begins asking questions about the text, in addition to her frequent questions about the story's plot or the characters in the narrative. Instead of turning the page before you are finished reading it, she may now wait for a moment and then ask whether you have finished yet. This is another sign of her rapidly increasing understanding of print. ❖

*Enjoying one of her favorite storybooks with some furry friends, this child is imitating what she has seen her teacher do at nursery school. Children who are read to frequently and who see adults enjoying books rarely have trouble learning to read.*

# The Incredible Journey to Literacy

No matter how much you read to her, your youngster will not all of a sudden become a reader. Before she can begin to read, she must develop the cognitive skills that will make it possible for her to perform such abstract tasks as categorizing letters and sounds, and generalizing the rules of spelling and language usage, an enormous task. She acquires these cognitive skills over time by experiencing her world firsthand. Exploring her environment with all her senses, she forms mental images of objects and, at the same time, makes some educated guesses about how things work. As her horizons broaden, she continually revises her concepts to fit newly acquired information.

Cognitive development will vary from child to child, with some children learning to read at an earlier age than others. But generally speaking, the ability to recognize that letters correspond to sounds, that a single letter can stand for several sounds, and that a single sound can be represented by several letters requires a level of reasoning that most children do not reach until they are six or seven, however intelligent they may be. That is why reading specialists recommend that reading not be formally taught until school age. Reading requires both cognitive sophistication and considerable experience with spoken and written language.

Just how fast a youngster becomes a reader depends on two unique factors — her inherited traits and her well of knowledge. Thus one child may teach himself to read at the age of four, while another, though she may be equally intelligent and verbal, will not learn until the second half of first grade.

To appreciate the remarkable progress that your youngster makes in the development of literacy in just a few short years, consider that a baby lacks an understanding of even the simple fact that people and objects continue to exist when they disappear from her sight. By the age of six, the same child not only knows that things exist apart from her, but that they can be represented by graphic symbols printed on a page.

*Pointing to a word on a page, a three-year-old is asking, "Mommy, what does this mean?" He is showing an increasing interest in print and is learning that the printed and spoken word can correspond.*

The wonderful moment when a child makes the connection between the spoken and written word can occur unexpectedly. Your youngster may look up from her play one day to see you sitting at the kitchen table writing down a list of grocery items. She comes over to you and asks you to read what is on the paper. When you have finished reading the list to her, she says, "Show me where it says milk." Her request indicates that she has learned that spoken words have written equivalents. Next, she asks to see where the list says apple juice. When you tell her apple juice is not on the list, she asks you to write it down "so we know we should buy some when we go to the store." Plainly she now understands that print functions in a very practical way: Its permanence serves to remind people later of things that they might otherwise forget.

The child who makes such a breakthrough in her thinking and discovers the function of print has probably begun to discover the mechanics of it, too. She may know, for example, that letters have physical properties and are made up of straight lines and curves, in different combinations.

By the age of four, she may have progressed so far as to be able to recognize and write her own name, recite the alphabet, and reproduce some of its letters, as well as read several words in context, such as the name of her favorite soft drink emblazoned across a billboard. But she will still have trouble recognizing words out of context. While your child may have no problem identifying the name of the cereal she eats when she sees it in brightly colored letters on the box, she may draw a blank when you show her the same word printed on a piece of paper. Even if you offer her the clue that it is what she had for breakfast that day, she is as likely to guess *cereal* as the correct word.

The child's error serves to illustrate a key difference between oral and written language. When you hand your child her stuffed bear and identify it as a bear, your youngster can easily relate the word *bear* to the object in her hand. Similarly, if she learns to associate the name of a fast-food chain with its logo, the logo is the visual clue that enables her to identify the word. To identify the word out of context, however, requires knowing something about how sounds and letters correspond, knowledge she does not yet have. Learning to read is the process of becoming able to recognize words by their visual clues as well as by their context.

In their first experiences with books, children have little notion of what reading involves. It is only natural that they assume the pictures tell the story. The title of a Dr. Seuss book, *I Can Read with My Eyes Shut!,* makes the point. Though most preschoolers are aware that books tell a story — and may even know parts of the story by heart — many do not yet realize that reading involves attending to the print on the page.

After a parent has finished reading aloud a well-loved tale, a child may grab the book and say, "Now I want to read it." Taking cues from the pictures, she reconstructs the story from memory. She usually delivers the story in a conversational style — a sign that she is not yet aware of text. Her retelling of "Goldilocks and the Three Bears," for example, might begin something like this: "Well, there were three bears. And they lived in the woods. And the mother made them this porridge. That's kind of like cereal. Oops! I forgot to tell you — there was a Papa Bear and a Baby Bear too. The porridge was hot so it burned them. Then they went for a walk. This girl came and her name was Goldilocks . . ."

The child's notion that a book may be read without looking at it, or by looking only at the pictures, gradually gives way to the realization around the age of three that somehow the text tells the story. She may still look at the pictures for clues to meaning, but her recounting of the story now begins to resemble written text in tone. At this point, her rendition of "The Three Bears" would probably sound more like: "Once upon a time there were three bears: a Papa Bear, a Mama Bear and a Baby Bear. They lived in a small house in the woods far, far away. One day, the Mama Bear made them some porridge, but it was too hot. So they went for a walk in the woods while it cooled off . . ."

A child familiar with a book filled with memory cues such as rhyme and repetition may be able to recite the book almost verbatim. And if she mistakenly deviates from her memorized version of the story, she will probably go back and correct herself. Such recounting from memory, of course, is not reading, at least from an adult's perspective. But it represents yet another milestone passed. It suggests that the child has learned that a book has a specific story and that the story does not change at each reading. It also shows that she now associates the story with the words written on the page, rather than pictures.

Interestingly, in the stage of development that follows, a child may realize that reciting from memory is not reading after all and refuse to do it when asked, saying, "I don't really know how." To many parents, this seems like a step backward. Actually, it is a significant step forward. It shows that the youngster is now aware that reading requires looking at the print to see the exact words there. She has correctly surmised that it involves matching speech to print, not reciting verbatim from memory.

**Waking up to print**   Long before he becomes aware of how speech and print correlate, your youngster may begin to display interest in figuring out how print works. At first he may sweep his finger back and forth across the words as he has seen readers do, unaware that the text is related closely to what is being said. Once he senses that speech and print correspond, he may try to match what he sees to what he hears. He may think that each letter stands for a syllable, assuming in the title "Three Little Pigs," for example, that the first four letters in the word *three* stand for the title's four syllables. But, puzzled by all the leftover letters, he will eventually revise his theory, perhaps this time thinking that each group of letters separated by space represents a syllable. Now the *three* works, but *little,* with its two syllables, will require him to use up the remaining two letter groups, leaving him nothing to point to when he comes to *pigs.* This trial-and-error process is known as print mapping and it generally goes on for several months before a child correctly perceives the connection between letters and sounds.

Once your youngster realizes that words are recognizable by their graphic symbols, he will begin to focus on one or two aspects of a word, such as its first letter. He may recognize parts of words that resemble his own name. A child named Dan might see the word *dandelion* and point to it saying, "There's my name!" Or he might notice the *an* in *man* and say, "That word is almost like Dan."

Equipped now with the understanding that letters and sounds are essentially one and the same, he will

*Sounding just like Papa Bear, this little girl wants to know, "Who's been sleeping in my bed?" Dialogue and the tonal differences between written and spoken language are becoming increasingly clear to her.*

enjoy games that involve rhyming and alliteration. Give him a word and tell him to begin a rhyme sequence — it will result in a long list of real and nonsense words that will amuse you both. These verbal exercises, which involve sorting words into their phonological, or sound, segments, form the basis of decoding and spelling. It often takes a long time, however, for children to progress from auditory discrimination of sounds to knowing which letters are associated with the sounds. Your child may be adept at rhyming a series of words, such as *can, man, pan, tan,* but if you show him the words written on a piece of paper, and even help him distinguish the initial sound of each, he still may not comprehend that the letters *a* and *n* represent the same sound in each. Despite the lag between hearing the differences and distinguishing them in print, a sensitivity to sound serves children well when they later receive formal reading instruction in school. Researchers have found that children who can distinguish the nonrhyming word from a list of several words read aloud to them later become better readers than those who cannot make the distinction.

**Learning through play**

Play, whether nonsense rhyming, pretending to read to an assembled menagerie of stuffed animals, or scribbling a map to a pirate's hidden treasure, is your child's most natural way of learning about written language. In play he practices what he has watched others do as they read and write, experimenting with the process and the product. With almost adultlike diligence, they amuse themselves endlessly, forming letters, manipulating them, combining them, all the while gaining insights into how these work to produce stories or convey ideas.

Even without letters to play with, youngsters would still learn something about how symbols work, an important concept when it comes to reading. Child experts believe there is a direct relationship between the symbolic representation in make-believe play and in reading. The boy, for example, who pretends his hand is an airplane by looping it up and down and around in the air is using it as a symbol, just as words are used as symbols in written language. Because he knows that his hand is not a real airplane, but only represents one, he will be better able to understand when it comes time to learn how to read that words can also stand for objects.

Play itself enhances a child's emerging literacy in other ways as well. A young child who is pretending to do the weekly shopping for the family checks his make-believe list as he pushes a plastic cart around the kitchen, picking from grocery items placed on the floor by his mother. Through such adventures in the world of make-believe, the youngster reinforces his understanding of the significance of the printed word.

When the many milestones on the way to reading that children pass during the preschool stage are reckoned, it is clear that their play and probing of their world have been anything but frivolous. The curiosity and imagination that served them so well will continue to give them motivation as they begin exploring the world of books on their own. ❖

*Although he is arranging books to make an airport for his toys, this youngster suddenly finds himself entranced when a volume falls open to a page full of dinosaurs — and a new dimension is added to his playtime.*

# Potential Problems

As a physiological act, reading begins with the eyes — with the visual messages that are flashed to the brain and interpreted there. Less obvious, but equally significant, is the role that hearing plays. The ability of the brain to differentiate from a welter of noise those sounds that constitute language is fundamental not only to speech but to reading and writing as well.

Thus, an impairment of either of these faculties increases the chances that a child will experience difficulty in learning to read. Even a temporary distress can interfere with his acquisition of language, making it harder for him to grasp the meaning of print. As a rule, however, minor problems of vision and hearing can be corrected with proper medical attention before a youngster falls too far behind.

**Hearing and language**

Since reading involves translating written words into their spoken counterparts, it stands to reason that any hitch in the development of oral language can have a negative effect on the process. In rare cases, a child may suffer a hearing loss due to permanent damage to the inner ear or the nerves connecting the ear to the brain. Such an impairment is almost certain to affect the child's speech, language development, and his ability to read, but in many cases may be compensated for with proper remedial support.

More common are hearing impairments caused by temporary blockages of the Eustachian tube, the small passageway connecting the back of the throat and the middle ear, just behind the eardrum. The blockage, in turn, causes otitis media, an inflammation of the middle ear. The inflammation can interfere with the vibration of the small bones in the middle ear when sound waves hit the eardrum, producing a hearing loss. While about 75 percent of all children have had at least one ear infection by the age of ten, some unlucky youngsters seem to get them regularly. Ear infections usually occur during the first six to seven years of life, when the Eustachian tube, which normally drains the middle ear and equalizes air pressure there, is nearly horizontal and can easily become blocked with fluids. As a child grows older and his head and neck mature, the Eustachian tube shifts to a more vertical position and thus permits better drainage.

Studies have shown that a youngster who suffers a first ear infection before the age of one has a considerably greater chance of having the condition become chronic. In later years, infections are most common among children subject to frequent colds or allergies and among children in day care, who are

## Symptoms That May Need Addressing

Hearing and vision problems that remain undetected and untreated for a long period of time may affect a youngster's later reading proficiency. You should consult your physician if your little one complains of hearing or vision problems or exhibits any of the following symptoms:

### Hearing

- Shows no response to loud noises by six months of age.
- Says no recognizable words by the age of eighteen months.
- Talks too loudly in normal conversation.
- Speaks in a monotone, with poor pronunciation.
- Does not speak in short sentences by the age of three.
- Turns one ear toward you.
- Does not respond to simple directions.
- Often asks you to repeat things.
- Turns up the volume too loud on a TV, record player, or cassette recorder.
- Rubs his ear repeatedly or complains of an earache.
- Has frequent colds, ear discharges, and upper respiratory infections.

### Vision

- Squints or rubs her eyes frequently.
- Often stumbles over small objects that are in plain view.
- Complains of frequent headaches, especially after looking at books or watching television.
- Complains of blurred vision or double vision.
- Closes one eye or cocks her head while looking at a book.
- Holds a book too close to her face or at arm's length.
- Complains that print is hazy or that it appears to be fading.
- Appears not to focus her eyes together on a single object.
- Cannot recognize at a distance objects that you can easily distinguish.

regularly exposed to youngsters suffering from upper respiratory infections. The loss of hearing caused by a middle-ear infection is usually only temporary, with normal hearing returning after the child has received medical treatment. But fluid can remain in the ear for weeks or even months, and this poses a danger. The child may exhibit only subtle symptoms that you may not associate with an ear infection; he may seem inattentive, misunderstand directions, or pull or scratch his ears. In fact, he may be experiencing a hearing loss that may interfere significantly with his language development. The critical period for beginning language skills is the first three years of a youngster's life, and so it is important that parents become especially aware during this time of the symptoms that point to a chronic reduction of hearing.

If your child is prone to long-term or recurrent ear infections, or if he shows any other symptoms of hearing loss *(box, above),* be sure to consult your pediatrician, who may refer you to an audiologist, or hearing specialist. In most cases, with early detection and treatment, you need not worry that your youngster's language skills will be permanently affected.

**Vision and reading**    As important to reading development as the ears are, the eyes have an even greater role to play. All babies are born slightly farsighted. This is because their eyeballs are relatively small, with the distance between the cornea and the retina too short for nearby images to focus clearly on the retina. Almost always, the condition corrects itself during infancy. As the toddler's vision continues to develop, his acuity at the age of two is approximately 20/70, which means that he sees at twenty feet what someone with normal vision sees at seventy feet. Although his eyes continue to be small, the lens is soft and able to accommodate and focus normally. Usually, by the age of six, the child's vision is a normal 20/20.

While a certain amount of farsightedness is part of a child's growth and development, nearsightedness, in which only objects close by can be seen clearly, is not normal and will require prescription eyeglasses. Astigmatism, a defect on the lens that causes blurry vision, can also develop during the preschool years and can be corrected by glasses.

Many infants lack the muscle control needed to focus both eyes together on an object. As a result, they appear to be cross-eyed. This condition generally corrects itself over time and need not be of concern unless it persists well past the age of six months. Amblyopia, or lazy eye, in which one eye focuses on an object while the other wanders in a different direction because of weaker muscles, is a potentially more serious condition. Unless it is treated, it may eventually cause blindness in the weaker eye. But if it is detected early, it can be cured by special exercises or by having the youngster wear a patch over the stronger eye, forcing him to use the weaker one and strengthen its muscles.

In most cases, a child who is having trouble with his eyes will complain or show symptoms that parents can recognize *(box, page 27).* But in some cases, the parents may attribute such symptoms as headaches or rubbing the eyes to tiredness or other factors when, in fact, these may be signs of trouble. Your child's vision should be screened annually as part of his regular medical checkup. Children who do show signs of difficulty should see an ophthalmologist for a more complete examination.

A child's general health can be an important factor in her learning to read. Children who are poorly nourished, tired, or frequently ill are often less motivated and attentive. A healthy, active, curious child brings a host of remembered experiences to reading. Her motor skills, for example, while not directly involved in reading, enable her to come successfully to grips with her environment, something that in itself is essential to her reading development.

Like physical health, a child's emotional state and social adjustment also affect her ability to read. Severe illness or tension in a household can reduce her powers of concentration and her immediate desire to learn. The youngster who is fully sound both in mind and body has a better chance of becoming a fluent reader.

**When reading difficulties appear**

Once a child enters elementary school, lurking reading problems may surface. Teachers may notice that a youngster stumbles in his reading or reads much more slowly than other children of his age. He may also have difficulty understanding and remembering what he has just read. Over time, his reading ability may remain significantly below grade level. Parents and peers, in turn, may perceive him as being less intelligent than he really is. And the youngster's frustration with the difficulties he is having may lead to behavioral problems or lower his self-esteem still further.

Often, such problems can be traced to poor health, emotional immaturity, family disturbances, or lack of support at home for reading and writing. In other cases, the reading method being used may not be best suited to the child's learning style. Sometimes, though, a child of average or above-average intelligence who suffers from none of these problems may still experience extreme difficulty in learning to read. If that is the case, he may be dyslexic *(box, page 30)*, a condition about which much remains to be learned.

Dyslexic children often are helped when attention is paid to their general language skills. Researchers have found that poor readers are often poor listeners, unable to comprehend readily what they hear. The inability of dyslexic youngsters to listen effectively can be especially damaging as they reach the upper grades, in which lectures are often given during class. Activities that enrich their vocabularies improve both their reading and listening skills.

Like many beginning readers, dyslexic children have trouble differentiating the individual sounds making up words. A child who cannot readily identify the odd word in a set such as *cat, sat, bat,* and *fad,* for example, is not hearing the individual sounds in

# An Expert's View

## Dyslexia: No Real Answers Yet

Dyslexia is a term used to describe the extraordinary difficulties some children of average or above-average intelligence have in learning to read.

For years, the condition was attributed mainly to deficiencies in visual perception, an inability to perceive correctly the words on the page. This theory was based on a number of characteristics common among dyslexics: unusual misspellings; the tendency to reverse letters and words, such as *b* for *d,* or *tar* for *rat;* mirror writing, in which whole sentences are written backward; and sloppy handwriting thought to be caused by an uncertain preference for left- or right-handedness. (Other indications of dyslexia are troubles in following print from left to right and a tendency to jump from one line to another.)

More recent research, however, suggests that dyslexia may result not from visual difficulties but from language problems caused by a dysfunction in the way the brain stores and retrieves information coded linguistically. Imagine the mind as an extremely sophisticated reference library. Even before a new library book is put on the shelf, it has to be catalogued: The book's title, a reference number, what it is about, and other subjects it is related to are entered on a card and filed in a card catalogue. Unfortunately, if the information is not recorded, or if it is recorded incorrectly, retrieving the book becomes very difficult.

The mind processes information in a similar manner. When a sensory stimulus, such as a letter or a word, enters the brain, an encoded version of it goes first to a short-term memory system where it is transformed into an abstract symbolic representation for storage in the brain's long-term memory. If the eye sees a *b* but the message is encoded as a *d,* a faulty representation is sent to the brain's long-term memory, or card file. As in the library, accurate retrieval is extremely difficult.

In one study, we asked groups of normal and dyslexic readers to print Hebrew words and letters in proper sequence after seeing them for a brief time. Neither group was familiar with Hebrew, which is sequenced from right to left. We found that the normal readers had as much difficulty with the task as the poor readers. We concluded that the recall of visual symbols representing words depends on familiarity with the linguistic properties of the words, in particular their meanings, their names, and the sounds of their letters.

In the course of reading a text, a reader can use two distinct strategies: He can either read a whole word at once by looking at its visual features and the context in which it appears, or he can break the word down into letters or units of sound, called phonemes. Normal youngsters beginning to read have no difficulty learning to use both strategies. Studies of dyslexic readers, however, have found that they generally have a poor grasp of letter sounds and phoneme values and tend not to use this strategy. They also have trouble remembering whole words.

As a result, words are stored without complete phonological, or name, codes — file cards in the library model. When a child is asked to call up a word, he finds that he does not have enough information to retrieve it. This may help explain why children classified as dyslexic — as many as 15 percent of American students — often have poorly developed vocabularies even before they learn to read. Dyslexics may also have difficulty using grammatic construction and syntax to aid their comprehension of meaning, and hence they may have trouble understanding what they read.

The underlying causes of dyslexia are still a mystery. Some researchers believe that dyslexia is due to genetic factors. It is more common in children with family histories of learning disorders, and boys are four to ten times more likely to have reading problems than are girls. Other studies have linked dyslexia to a maturational lag, in which neither the left nor the right hemisphere of the brain dominates the development of language; normally, the brain's left hemisphere controls spoken and written language and verbal reasoning skills.

A number of researchers believe that the reading problems associated with dyslexia are caused by minimal brain dysfunction (MBD), in which there is neurological impairment in the areas of the brain that control language and memory functions. Still other researchers argue that there are many possible causes of dyslexia, based on evidence that children classified as dyslexic show deficiencies in a variety of basic processes. They say that more study into a wide range of reading disorders is necessary before their origins can be pinpointed.

The longstanding belief that dyslexia is caused by deficiencies in visual perception has led to widespread use of vision therapy as treatment. Vision therapy includes eye exercises, movement exercises designed to improve eye-hand coordination, and the prescription of eyeglasses. As new studies cast doubt on the role of visual perception in dyslexia, however, the benefits of vision therapy are being seriously questioned.

Instead, most experts now believe that the best way of helping dyslexic children is to provide them with individual tutoring and remedial programs aimed at reinforcing both whole-word identification and phonetic decoding skills, as well as comprehension of meaning. Such programs should be accompanied by activities to enrich the vocabularies of dyslexic children and enhance their awareness of language sounds.

*Frank R. Vellutino, Ph.D.*
*Professor of Psychology and Director, Child Research*
*and Study Center, The University at Albany*

the words distinctly. Activities such as rhyming games that give him practice in hearing the separate sounds will increase his awareness of the way speech is structured.

The intricacies of complex sentences, not surprisingly, offer dyslexic children particular problems. Opportunities for hearing and reading ever more complex sentences can increase skill in deciphering them. Researchers have discovered that children who are able to listen to the reading of a text while following along in the book comprehend the material better than they do by reading or listening alone.

Unfortunately, not all teachers pick up on the possibility of dyslexia or another learning disability and often attribute the difficulties of youngsters experiencing them to a variety of factors, including family upsets.

Being able to predict reading problems during a child's early years would obviously be of great benefit. As yet, specialists have had little success in accurately predicting any but the most severe reading problems. There are, however, some general clues. A child's language development appears to be the best indicator of his future reading skill. Children whose language development is abnormally slow, who are not using recognizable words by eighteen months, or who are not speaking in short sentences by the age of three are more likely to have reading problems once they enter school. Other more subtle signs, such as a four-year-old's inability to distinguish rhyming words or his lack of interest in playing nonsense rhyming games, might also indicate a mild hearing loss that is interfering with his language development. If your child's language development lags significantly behind that of other children his age, your pediatrician can refer your youngster to a speech-language pathologist for complete evaluation and therapy. With early intervention many delays in the development of your child's language skills can be remedied.

Other signs of potential problems are less accurate predictors, but they are worth noticing. A child who shows little interest in attempting to read and write during the preschool years may later have difficulty reading. Certain behavior characteristics, such as hyperactivity and an inability to concentrate, may also predict reading problems ahead.

Whatever his age and whatever his problem, a youngster responds best to the kind of nurturing, individual, low-key encouragement that can be best provided by loving, supportive parents. ❖

# Steps along the Way

Children interact with books in a variety of ways, as they move along the path to literacy. This chart follows the sequence of young children's book behaviors through four categories: picture reading, book handling, story and book comprehension, and story reading.

Picture reading demonstrates the ways in which children react to the illustrations in books, from the rapt gazing of the infant, to the toddler's quest for the names of pictured objects, to the four-year-old's use of the pictures as cues in reciting a memorized story. Book handling traces changes in the child's physical manipulation of the book, as her growing abilities let her understand, more and more, what a book is.

Story and book comprehension lists the behaviors that show the youngster's dawning awareness that each book contains a given story, and that books have things in common with one another and with events in her life. Story reading outlines the process by which the child connects spoken words and print, starting with her babbling in the presence of a familiar book and winding up with her realization that the book tells the reader what words to say — that the story is in fact in the print and that the letters tell how the words sound.

The chart indicates the ages at which children begin to display these various kinds of book behavior. As youngsters move toward literacy they will exhibit most of the reactions listed on these four pages, but they may not adhere strictly to the sequence or to the timespans given. Thus when consulting the chart, remember, as always, that your child may differ somewhat from the norm spelled out here.

## Picture Reading

- Looks at pictures intently, especially those that are simple, bold, and bright. (2 to 4 months)

- After several months of handling, chewing, and tearing books, returns to looking at pictures. (8 to 10 months)

- Points to pictures. (8 to 12 months)

- Laughs or smiles at a familiar picture, especially one for which the adult makes an interesting or playful sound. (8 to 12 months)

- Can name objects depicted, or point to one of them when asked, "Where's the . . .?" (10 to 14 months)

- Not only points to objects pictured, but asks for names, saying, "What's that?" or "Dat?" (13 to 20 months)

- Pats pictures of things liked. (15 to 18 months)

- Pretends to pick up objects pictured on pages; for example, scoops jam from a pictured jam jar and then gleefully puts fingers in mouth (left). (2 to 2½ years)

- Using illustrations as cues, "reads" memorized book aloud. (3 to 4 years)

# Book Handling

- Looks at pictures, but does not touch. (2 to 4 months)

- Brings book to the mouth to investigate by sucking and chewing. (5 to 10 months)

- Deliberately tears paper pages, if they are offered *(below, left)*. (5 to 15 months)

- After one reading, takes book from adult and requests second reading by handing it back. (8 to 10 months)

- Sits for 10 minutes or more to look at books; does much more looking and less handling. (8 to 12 months)

- Turns pages awkwardly. (8 to 12 months)

- Tears pages accidentally, because of difficulty in holding or manipulating books, but stops tearing them intentionally. (12 to 14 months)

- Turns pages relatively well. Flips through a book by gathering a clump of pages and then letting them fly past. (11 to 15 months)

- Turns an inverted book right side up or turns head, trying to see picture right side up. (11 to 15 months)

- Confronting a picture of something that is upside down *(above, left)*, may rotate book until pictured object is upright. If upright picture on facing page is now upside down, may keep rotating book; becomes frustrated and loses interest. (16 to 20 months)

- Knows difference between a book that is upside down and one in which something upside down is pictured. Rotates book only briefly or not at all. (2 years)

- Can point to top or bottom of page; can turn to front or back of book when asked. (2½ to 3 years)

- Becomes aware of graphic elements that mark the start of a new chapter in a book with many sections. (4 to 5 years)

# Story and Book Comprehension

- Laughs or smiles at picture, as if to indicate recognition. (8 to 12 months)

- Relates object or action in book to real world; touches own shoe, for example, after seeing shoes pictured in book. (10 to 14 months)

- Selects books on basis of their content, thus showing understanding of what book is about; picks up book with picture of truck in it, for example, after playing with toy truck. (10 to 15 months)

- Shows special understanding or enjoyment of favorite page by searching through book for it or by repeatedly holding the book open at that page. (11 to 14 months)

- Performs action that is shown or mentioned in book; for example, wants to feed milk to kitten after reading about it. (12 to 23 months)

- Shows empathy for characters or situations depicted in books; for example, pretends to cry after being told that child shown in book is sad. (16 to 20 months)

- Makes associations with other books; goes and gets second book about puppies after reading one about puppies, or gets two books and shows that they contain similar pictures or events. (20 months)

- Has favorite book. (18 to 24 months)

- Talks about characters and events in storybooks, in way that reveals understanding of story; relates events in books to own experiences. (20 to 26 months)

- Remains attentive as story is read aloud, even when pictures are not visible. (3 to 4 years)

# Story Reading

- Vocalizes at first unintelligibly, while pointing to a picture. Makes appropriate animal or other sounds (such as "choo-choo") when looking at familiar pictures. (10 to 13 months)

- Uses book babble: While looking at book, chatters in nonsense sounds, but with intonations of reading rather than conversation. (13 to 14 months)

- Shows awareness of print in books, for instance, by pointing to labels under pictures while adult names them. (15 to 20 months)

- Fills in next word in the text when adult pauses, or recites text along with adult. (15 to 28 months)

- Says part of text on page as soon as page is turned; seeing pictures, knows what page says. (17 months)

- "Reads" to dolls or stuffed animals. (17 to 25 months)

- Recites storybook text while away from story-reading setting, for example, when swinging. (21 months)

- Recites whole phrases of favorite stories, if adult pauses during story-reading. (24 to 30 months)

- Protests when adult misreads familiar (usually predictable) story; supplies correct word. (25 to 27 months)

- Asks to read books to adult and may be able to recite passages from predictable or familiar books fairly accurately. (28 to 34 months)

- Moves finger or whole hand across line of print and recites what it says, giving exact text or accurate paraphrase. (32 months)

- Tells story of familiar book by describing pictures in own words. (2 to 3 years)

- Tells story of familiar book while looking at illustrations, but using language closely resembling that found in book. (4 to 5 years)

- Tries to read familiar story by paying attention to print. (5 to 6 years)

# 2 An Urge to Write

As with reading, writing is attempted at a surprisingly early age. Some babies discover the pleasures of scribbling before they reach their first birthdays, and the unadulterated joy of making marks on a page continues to grow with each passing day. It moves children to put pen or crayon to paper throughout their preschool years. By the time they are three, they clearly distinguish between scribbles that are drawing and ones that are writing. And as they watch you write — whether it is checks at the bank counter, notes to your friends, or lists for the grocery store — they are inspired to probe deeper into this very adult-seeming magic.

The processes by which children learn to write and read are complementary. The perceptions children form while scrawling on paper shed light on their early impressions of reading. The converse is also true. They notice examples of written and printed words just about everywhere they turn. Dauntlessly, they begin to imitate these examples. Like scientific researchers on the trail of a laboratory breakthrough, they work methodically to improve their understanding of how writing works and what they can do with it. Educators have found that such trial-and-error learning is remarkably consistent from one child to the next everywhere in the world.

Early in this self-directed education, children make a crucial connection: Writing is an activity with a purpose. Those odd-looking marks their parents produce convey meaning to others. Fired by their new understanding, they now have a concrete goal driving their experiments forward. Long before the girl at right will be able to turn out a readable thank-you note, she writes one as best she can and will happily read it to anyone who will listen. From now on, there will be no stopping her. Although the letters may not form recognizable words, already she proudly thinks of herself as a writer.

# Twinned Skills: Reading and Writing

Learning to read and learning to write are so closely related that one really cannot happen without the other. Researchers studying youngsters who discover how to read before entering school have found that they are usually "paper and pencil kids." These children begin by scribbling and drawing, and then they move on to copying letters of the alphabet from their storybooks and other examples of adult writing. Later the children attempt to create words on their own and compare their efforts to the words they find printed in books and on signs and food cartons. These children also ask lots of questions about spelling. Finally, they teach themselves to read.

Even with less precocious children, it is the insights they gain playing with paper and pencil that help them make sense of the words they see on a page. It is also their curiosity about the words they notice — on signs, in newspaper headlines, on the sides of big trucks, anywhere they find print — that makes it possible for them to progress as writers and readers as well.

**Grasping the form and function of writing**

For preschoolers, experimenting with writing requires two distinct sets of new skills. First, the youngster must begin to grasp the fundamentals of handwriting. He must make an effort to master the assortment of symbols that make up the alphabet —

fifty-two letters in all, twenty-six of them uppercase, twenty-six lowercase — along with a handful of punctuation marks. At the same time, he has to develop an ability to compose messages — to use written language as a communication tool. In other words, the child must learn both the form and the function of writing.

In the years before starting school, children make considerable progress in these directions on their own. Indeed, before becoming skilled in either area — and long before learning to read — it is not uncommon for them to think of themselves as writers already. Often, youngsters begin with the bold assumption that the first haphazard squiggles they make actually communicate messages to other people. Although the expectations of these young would-be writers are wildly optimistic, the children have awakened to the fact that writing is done for a purpose. They begin to understand that written language is meant to connect them with others and to convey their thoughts.

On an equally fundamental level, children soon come to realize that writing and speaking are altogether different ways of communicating. For one thing, the writer and the reader, unlike the speaker and the listener, may be far apart in time and space. A birthday greeting mailed on Monday may not reach

Suitably unfazed by the irregularities in her spelling, this five-year-old writes and illustrates a story about losing her tooth on Christmas Eve. Because she is familiar with the event, she is able to enjoy the sensation of being a fluent reader. Her experience at the drawing board will help build confidence for trying to read other people's writing.

its destination or convey its message until the end of the week. A story that was written a hundred years ago may still be fun to hear read aloud this evening. From these glimpses into the nature of writing and from frequent exposure to printed words, youngsters gradually comprehend that written messages have a unique set of requirements and functions. They begin to sense that their own writing will have to fall in step with the way grownups write. And as time goes by, they come to the understanding that writing somehow has to express its meaning without the personal contact that exists in spoken conversation.

Just as there are lessons to be learned about the differences between speaking and writing, there is a crucial discovery to be made about the way that the two are related. Although children at first do not understand that the letters of the alphabet represent sounds, they obviously have to make the connection if their writing is to be more than mere memorized combinations of letters. They also have to learn many characteristics of formal writing that are nothing more than conventions. Some of these, such as the way that spaces are used to separate individual words, are usually learned through the child's own observations. Others, such as certain intricacies of English spelling, will not fall into place for a long time.

**Learning by doing**

As is the case with many other skills acquired in early childhood, writing is best learned by doing. The very act of playing with markers and paper perfectly fulfills a youngster's need to explore things with her hands, her eyes, and her ears, and to have an effect — to leave her mark, as it were. She finds both the process and the product intrinsically enjoyable. In a very real sense, the pleasure the youngster derives when she scrawls across reams of paper, learns to make the shapes of letters, and later starts to create her own written messages is all the motivation she needs.

Children begin writing the same way they begin speaking, by imitating adults. Just as a child's first babbling attempt at vocalization bears only a crude resemblance to the speech of her parents, her earliest writing is made up of scribbles that barely approximate the real thing. But like babbling, which has the music if not the words of oral language, her early scrawl already has some of the form, without the function, of written language. Throughout a youngster's preschool years her writing, like her speech, will make enormous strides toward approximating the examples of written language she observes around her.

**Moving from the whole to the parts**

Even when your very young writer seems to be doing little more with the markers than joyfully expressing herself, she is adding to her general fund of understanding about what is involved in the process of writing. At first, she is more fascinated with the overall appearance of writing than with its particular details. She perceives writing as a whole, as a never-ending string of shapes, rather than as a product of many individual letters or words.

This perspective is a little difficult for an adult to comprehend; it seems obvious that if a youngster is to learn to write, she would have to memorize the letters and figure out how to put them together to make words and sentences. For preschoolers, however, the process is exactly the other way around. Their basic approach is to move from an understanding of the whole to an understanding of the parts — from general impressions of what writing is to the particulars. In actual fact, this approach is typical of the ways young children learn about many other things as well, speaking and reading included.

In her first attempts to write, your youngster tries to capture the dominant features of writing, without being worried about the details *(box, pages 46-47)*. Eventually she discovers that writing is composed of many individual symbols. With her newfound knowledge, your little one starts to put down many separate marks on her paper. In time, she notices that there are differences between her marks and those on the printed page, and this drives her to try shaping them to conform to the models at hand.

**When squiggles turn into letters**

The wonderful discovery process that leads your child to replace her squiggles with the standard ABC's should be largely her own for it to be a well-learned and satisfying lesson. There is no need at this stage of your youngster's development to teach her the alphabet simply as a means of helping her learn to write. Preschoolers are quite utilitarian and choose to learn only what they really need to know. Your youngster will become her own best teacher as she forges ahead with her experiments. In her confident zeal, she does not regard the alphabet as a starting point. She is refreshingly innocent of what it means to be ignorant.

Your youngster's motives in learning to write are really quite simple: She wants to express herself and wants to have fun while she is doing so. Writing is nothing more than a useful means to an end.  ⁂

# Writing at Its Most Elemental

It all begins with scribbling. Young children do not need even pencil and paper to get started at this happy pastime — fingers are their most rudimentary marking tools. Strapped into a car seat, a youngster may stretch out her hand to rub swirls on the fogged-up window of the car. Seated in her high chair at mealtime, she will finger-paint with the food that spills on her tray. The artist's medium is inconsequential: She will doodle in the dust on a window sill, the dirt at the playground, or the sand at the beach. And if she gets hold of a crayon, she will happily adorn walls, floors, furniture, or any other surface she can reach. In her eagerness to scribble, she may even decorate her own limbs and clothing, as the toddler pictured at right is doing. It is in early scribbling adventures such as these that the magic of writing originates. Typically these adventures begin spontaneously, at around eighteen months of age. However, when children are specifically shown that a writing tool leaves a mark, they sometimes start experimenting as early as their first birthday.

**The value of scribbling**

Scribbling is not just fun; it is also a useful learning activity. As your child scribbles, she gains firsthand experience with all the different strokes that formal writing will require. Tilting and swerving her random scrawls around the page, she produces curved and straight lines, continuous marks and some that are broken, lines that run parallel and others that intersect. In short, she incorporates all the variables that she will use again later on when she forms real letters. Scribbling is not only a simple creative act that a youngster practices for its own sake, it is also a rehearsal for the more conventional forms of writing she will soon want to explore.

**Uncontrolled scribbling**

Researchers at one time believed that a youngster's earliest scribbling, which fills the page with uncontrolled lines, was nothing more than a way of exercising hands and arms. However, the experts have since discovered that it is the pleasure of leaving marks on the paper that is the principal attraction. The lines and swirls made by the child that appear on the page are the real rewards.

This fact was demonstrated in 1968, when researchers monitored the scribbling activities of a group of children ranging in age from fifteen to thirty-eight months. Each youngster was given paper and a pair of identical-looking writing tools, only one of which would actually produce marks on the paper. In every case, the children scribbled for long periods of time when they

were using the pens that worked, but quickly lost interest in the pens that left no marks. One sixteen-month-old, who had never before held a writing implement, started out waving the pen randomly. When it happened to strike and mark the paper, her attention was riveted immediately, and she began to scribble with abandon. She had discovered what writing specialists call the fundamental graphic act — the gesture that leaves a mark. Once a child has made this discovery, all subsequent writing progress is simply a matter of learning to control and refine that fundamental act.

**Controlled scribbling**
A child's initial, free-form scribbling may fill a page with back-and-forth lines or roughly circular markings. Once the young-ster has gained experience with pencil and paper, he advances to what is called controlled scribbling. Now the marks tend to become smaller and tighter than the earlier scribbles. They also begin to show deliberate patterns. Strokes may be ar-

ranged vertically, horizontally, or in circular patterns, and different kinds of marks may appear in clusters in different positions on the page.

If the child is allowed frequent use of his crayons, he soon begins producing two distinct types of marks: scribble drawings and scribble writing. Squiggles and curlicues that look like writing begin to be distinguishable from others that are obviously pictures. Sometimes these distinctions begin to emerge before the child is three years of age. At this stage the youngster is starting to reveal an awareness of certain characteristics of formal writing. On occasion, his scrawls and marks take on a linear, horizontal form. And just as adult writing uses a standard set of characters repeated in varying patterns, the youngster's scribbles begin to feature repetition of certain elements. The results may resemble either cursive writing or printing, depending upon his source or inspiration. In either case, the new control in his efforts indicates that the child has moved a step closer to actual written language.

**Discovering the features of print**
Between the ages of three and a half and four, as the youngster's controlled scribbling grows more refined, and he is increasingly exposed to books, newspapers, street signs, labels, and a multitude of other writings, he begins to experiment with shapes that look like parts of letters. All of the uppercase and lowercase letters in the Roman alphabet, used in written English and most European languages, are formed from ten basic components. There are dots; strokes arranged vertically, horizontally, and at opposite diagonals; closed loops; and loops that open facing up, down, left, and right. An *S,* for example, combines two loops — one facing left, the other right. An *A* is composed of one horizontal line and diagonals in both directions. An *O* is a closed loop, while a lowercase *f* combines a downward loop with vertical and horizontal lines. A lowercase *j* has a vertical line, an upward loop, and a dot. Before a child begins to be able to form

*Three preschoolers scribble with chalk on the sidewalk. The youngster at left focuses on a series of vertical lines. This typifies the stage called controlled scribbling. The other children are drawing pictures and exhibit somewhat more advanced skills. Whatever their level of ability, young children take innate pleasure in writing.*

actual letters, his writing incorporates some or all of these ten distinctive shapes.

**Mock letters** The next step in the youngster's progress is to add to his graphic repertoire so-called mock letters, which are letter-like shapes made up of the same basic lines, curves, and dots that compose real letters. The Roman alphabet does not use all the possible combinations of these component forms, and the child who is just beginning to write takes enormous pleasure in carrying out experiments with his own variations. Some children get so caught up in this game that they seem to reinvent the alphabet.

At this stage in writing development, your youngster is learning to pay attention to the smallest graphic components of written language — individual letters. He is beginning to look at an exit sign, for example, and recognize it not just as a single unified symbol, but as a combination of four separate symbols. Understanding how those four symbols work together to create a distinctive sound pattern is necessary in learning to read. For writing, however, your child also has to be able to deal with each of them physically — actually create them. As your youngster scribbles mock letters and grows ever more conscious of the real letters he sees all around him, you may see him playing with letters in various ways. He may color or decorate the outlines of letter shapes or turn printed words sideways and upside down to see how the letters change their appearance. He is making great strides as a writer and doing so in ways that he finds to be fun.

**First inklings of the forms of writing** As your child tinkers with the various physical characteristics of written language, she also exhibits a beginning awareness that writing takes different forms, depending on what needs to be communicated. She notices that shopping lists are long and narrow, which makes items easy to find and check off, while the text of stories, which are read in sequence so they make sense, stretches all the way across the page of a book. Personal letters also have a distinctive form and can be distinguished from other types of writing by the salutation at the beginning and the signature at the end. Elements of these various formats begin to find their way into your youngster's increasingly mature scribble writing. As with every aspect of her passage through the scribbling phase, her experiments with form are inspired by observations of the writing you do or the writing she sees performed by older children.  ∴

# Exploring Written Language

Once your child moves beyond scribbling and begins to form recognizable letters of the alphabet, he operates on a new level in exploring written language. Now the business at hand is to produce words, and the youngster approaches this challenge with the same curiosity and enthusiasm that carried him through the lessons of the scribbling phase. His understanding of words is nonexistent at first and needs a considerable period to evolve. By the time he reaches elementary school, however, he may already have taught himself to write combinations of letters that closely approximate real words.

To invent logical spellings without formal instruction, a child must make a number of important discoveries about the conventions and formalities of adult writing. But learning to write is not a neat, step-by-step progression. Rather, it is a process of discovery by doing, of gradually correcting imprecision. The moving force throughout this endeavor is the youngster's intuitive sense that he can make his writing more like that of adults if he simply keeps trying and compares his work to the words that he finds all around him. In this respect, his first successes in producing written words repeat his beginnings as a talker.

**Names as early visual models**
Both speaking and writing usually start with names. A baby's first spoken word is often *Mama* or *Dada.* Similarly,

---

## Milestones of Writing

**Uncontrolled Scribbling**

*A young toddler's first markings on paper are characterized by pure randomness. At this stage, the scribbles do no more than record hand movements across the page. More than anything, they express delight in the ability to produce marks on the paper.*

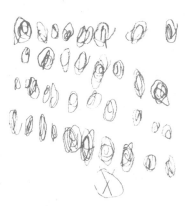

**Scribbling under Control**

*Although still more akin to a baby's scribbling than to legible words, these marks begin to show aspects of standard written English. They are arranged in horizontal rows and include one character from the alphabet — the circled X at the bottom.*

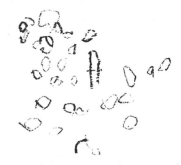

**Progressing to Mock Letters**

*This sample demonstrates a beginner's understanding of the kinds of marks used in writing. The A at center is the best reproduction of an actual letter. But several others of these so-called mock letters are similar to numbers or lowercase letters.*

when your child is old enough to begin writing, the first word he tries is generally a name — in most cases, his own. The desire to put his name on paper may be one of the strongest motivations for learning to write. Names hold special meaning for toddlers, who correctly think of them as almost-tangible labels carried about by their owners. When your youngster makes his own name tangible — by writing it down on paper — he establishes a familiar visual model of what writing needs to be and of what a word is.

At first he may know only one or two letters from watching you print his name for him. But that is enough for the time being: In his mind those couple of letters represent his name, the one word he thinks he can write. In some cases a child may know precisely how many letters his name has, even if he cannot write all of them. A boy named Jack, for example, may write a perfect *J* and follow it with three unrelated letters, one each for the *A, C,* and *K,* which he will recite aloud as he points to his substitute letters. He has the idea that several symbols are needed to write his name; he even knows how many. But he does not yet use the letters actually needed to write his name or realize that they are selected by the sounds they represent.

When he learns to produce a reasonable facsimile of his name, whether it is perfect or not, he may want to post it on his door,

**Early Practice at Name Writing**

*In one of two attempts, this child came close to correctly writing his name, David. The A is inverted but the rest is fine. Names are often the first words children try, but it takes time before they see that the direction of letters affects their meaning.*

**Combining Letters**

*Drawing strictly on characters from his name, Adam, this child has produced a letter-length block of text without filling it with scribbles or mock letters. He understands that writing involves repetition but knows that it demands variation as well.*

**Writing Mock Words**

*This child has begun to write mock words. She has grasped the notion that writing involves groups of letters in varied combinations, arranged horizontally. She is not yet aware, however, of the correspondence between written letters and spoken sounds.*

inscribe it on his toys, and emblazon it across every piece of his artwork. He may also want to learn to write the other names that figure in his world: yours, those of his siblings, relatives, pets, playmates, or even characters from books and television. Names are the most obvious and accessible way for him to do what you do when you write — make words.

**Writing mock words**
In the early stages of writing development, children also start trying to write words other than names. By the time she is four or five, your child's observations have told her that all writing is composed from a small group of recognizable symbols repeated over and over. Indeed, her awareness is what led her to practice forming the shapes of the alphabet in the first place. To some extent, her first attempts to make words flow from this knowledge. She may fill a page with repetitions of her name, her initial, or the first few letters that she has learned to write. Only later does she discover that unlimited repetition is not part of written language and that to communicate at all in writing, she must learn to repeat the symbols sparingly and within strict limits.

From such discoveries grows ever-greater awareness of writing's complexity. Eventually she will come to realize that while all words are made up from the same set of letters, the letters are rearranged in a multitude of different patterns. The tens of thousands of words in the English language can be generated from the small group of symbols contained in the alphabet. And a few hundred words can be arranged in different combinations to generate all the stories in her favorite books. These realizations lead your child beyond simple repetition and induce her to begin rearranging the letters in different configurations.

In the process she produces what are called mock words, experimental groupings of letters that have the form but not the meaning of real words. Mock words reflect your child's changing understanding of what makes a word. She has noticed that words contain several letters — often five or six — and that letters vary within a word and across different words. The mock words she writes on a page might include *AOALL, LOLOAA,* and *OALOA.* At this stage, she is operating on incomplete impressions about how writing works. She tests her new theories while playing writing games. She is, in effect, reinventing the rules that govern written language. She thus makes the system of written symbols her own, by mastering its underlying principles.

As she experiments, she first assumes that every new string of letters created is an authentic word. Hers may incorporate real letters, mock letters, and even numbers. She may run to you frequently with made-up words that she wants you to read: "Look, Mommy, I made *A-A-Q-L-Y.* What did I write?" Later, when she has heard too many of your tortured phonetic pronunciations and has been told several times, "That is not a word but you're getting close," she will realize that her visual approach to writing leaves something to be desired. At this point or soon after, she will begin to think about sounds as she writes. She will find that some combinations of letters are words while others are not. Earlier, writing mock letters helped her master the shapes of the alphabet. Now her games with mock words help her understand the qualities that real words must have.

**Making lists**    Beginning writers often make a game of producing spontaneous lists of the words and letters they are learning. In the process, they create systematic records of their written vocabularies — registering their mistakes along with their recognizable spellings. These games are enjoyable exercises that help children notice the common elements of the words they include on their lists. Just as they are learning that words have rules, they are

## Imprints of Culture

As soon as children make the distinction between writing and drawing, their scribbling begins to reflect the influences of their native tongue and its graphics. The three scribble-writing samples below reflect this point quite dramatically. The page on the left is by an American-born child from an English-speaking home, the one in the middle is by a Saudi Arabian, and the one on the right by an Israeli. All were four years old and classmates at an Indiana preschool that brings together children

from various cultures. They had been given this straightforward instruction: "Write everything you can write." Though illegible, the samples clearly capture the very different looks of the Roman, Arabic, and Hebrew alphabets. Children often have a surprising awareness of adult writing in their scribbling. When the Saudi child submitted her work, she warned the teacher: "You can't read it because it is in Arabic." She also said that Arabic uses "a lot more dots" than English.

**An American child**    **A Saudi Arabian child**    **An Israeli child**

likely to impose their own rules on the lists they devise. The earliest lists may be as simple as a series of individual letters or numbers. Older children may move on to lists that match letters with words that use them: *A Apple, F Fish, M Mommy,* and the like. Other lists will simply be inventories: all the words that the children know, all the animal names they know how to write, all the playmates they saw in the park today.

**Learning from differences and similarities**

Children's list making and experiments in writing mock words bring into focus the differences and similarities among letters and words. Some youngsters are fascinated by the contrast between uppercase and lowercase letters. They may compose lists of words written in both forms, so they can explore the differences in size and shape in the contrasting versions. Other children devote great care and effort to writing pairs of letters, such as *A* and *H,* which share certain common features but are different in other respects, or *b* and *d,* or *M* and *W,* which are reversals of each other. This interest in contrasts and similarities carries over to other areas, such as meaning and sound. Youngsters in kindergarten sometimes list pairs of rhyming words and pairs that are opposite in meaning. There is some evidence that such contrastive writing activities accelerate a youngster's progress at reading by obliging him to pay close attention to the distinctive details of individual letters and words. It is best to let children invent their own learning games, however, rather than giving them formal writing exercises to carry out.

**Writing in haphazard directions**

One requirement of adult writing that preschoolers have difficulty grasping is the need to write in a single direction only.

*To write this ticket for a preschool production of "The Three Little Pigs," a child has used both her early and recently acquired writing skills. She has copied the words from a sample written by an adult. The numbers at the top she wrote from memory, knowing that tickets usually have numbers on them. The three lines of scribbling are typical signs of a beginning writer who has space to fill but has grown tired of writing standard characters.*

## Letter Reversals and Mirror Writing

As children begin forming letters and words on their own, they introduce many deviations from the left-to-right, top-to-bottom orientation of standard writing. They may write individual letters backward or upside down, and they may even produce whole pages of mirror writing, with letters uniformly reversed and lines of text running from right to left. Some parents worry unnecessarily that these tendencies are signs of dyslexia *(box, page 30)* or other learning disabilities. Most often they are not that at all: They are simply the child's way of experimenting with written language and testing the limits of the system's flexibility.

Letters are among the few visual objects that change their identity when their orientation is changed. A picture of a cow does not change into a dog or a goat if it is turned upside down or backward. But if the letter *b* is flopped or rotated, it changes to a *d, p,* or *q.* It may take several years of writing experience for a youngster to master such concepts. Some children also find it hard to write from left to right while forming letters such as *C, G, J,* or *S,* which are made with a right-to-left stroke. Moreover, if the position of drawings or other writing on a page forces a youngster to begin a word near the right-hand edge, carrying on by arranging the letters from right to left may feel quite natural to him. Letter reversals and mirror writing usually disappear after the first few years of elementary school.

---

Youngsters learning to write English in school have to be taught to print consistently in horizontal, left-to-right rows, beginning at the top of the page and proceeding to the bottom. Most children have little use for such a rule when they first start to write. Their freewheeling sense of how words should be presented on the page is understandable, given their limited knowledge of standard writing conventions. Quirks such as writing upside down, backward, or turning words around corners when they reach the margins of a page are akin to the common beginner's tendency to omit all the spaces between words. The child knows perfectly well what he is trying to write, though the format he uses may not always indicate that. Only with experience does he learn the reasons for writing within the standard formats and acquire the skills he needs to do it.

**Associating sounds with writing**

Early in their explorations of writing, children begin to think about sounds as they try to write words. It is the first time they clearly associate the auditory and visual aspects of language. One way they reveal this awareness is through an approach to spelling called the syllabic hypothesis. A beginning writer will represent each syllable in a word with a single written letter; he will write one character to spell *dog,* for example, two for *baby,* and three for the word *tricycle.* Though he is noting the multiple sounds within words, he does not yet grasp that the letters denote particular sounds. When he writes the word *Daddy,* he may write the letter *J* and say, "Dad," then jot down a *T* and say, "dy." He is confident that he has written the entire word — but not for long. By testing this method with very familiar words, such as their own names, most children soon discover its shortcomings. A child named Matthew will notice that he is not using the many letters he has grown accustomed to seeing in his name if he uses just one letter for each of the two syllables.

Occasionally children experiment with other original theories on how to make words. They may assign very few letters to the words for things that are small — such as insects, birds, and children — and many letters to words for things that are larger, such as airplanes, grownups, and elephants. They have even been known to add letters to their names on birthdays, in charming celebration of another year's growth. More often, however, they simply begin to ask their mothers and fathers for spelling advice, especially after a few episodes of seeing long words, such as *caterpillar,* denoting small things, and small words, such as *car,* denoting large things.

One important insight comes when children listen to their parents say the sounds of letters while writing them, or when they watch their parents point to the letters of a word while pronouncing its sounds. The children begin to realize that individual letters match up with particular sounds. This is what researchers call phonemic awareness, and it is key to youngsters' further progress with writing and spelling.

**Invented spelling**  Once they understand that the letters in a word have a purpose, children begin to make words based on the sounds of specific letters. Their spelling will be far from standard as they put their new knowledge of sounds and letters to use. But in its own way, their spelling is logical and in many cases understandable to adults. At this point, children are able to read back many of the words that they write.

A child's earliest invented spellings typically concentrate on beginning and ending letters, with the intermediate vowels often omitted. This is especially true when the vowel sounds are short: A child may write *BK* for *book* and *FT* for *foot.* Through practice, he gradually fills in the vowels and assigns letters to all the sounds in a word. *Monster* may begin as *MSD,* then progress to *MOSTR* before the child achieves the correct spelling.

Perfect spelling of English, with its many silent letters and other peculiarities, will not come quickly, of course. But as your little one gains experience as a reader and writer, he begins more and more to compare his own spellings to those that he sees in print. In this self-correcting fashion, your youngster's reading and writing skills work together to sharpen his spelling and bring it into line with adult writing.   ❖

# From the Concrete to the Abstract

Two major communication skills, writing and drawing, emerge from a child's early scribbling. Although the two generally evolve together, some experts regard drawing as a preparatory step toward writing. They believe that pictures, which are less abstract than words, are easier for children to understand. A picture of Mommy, for example, stands for the real person, a tangible part of the child's world. The written word *Mommy,* on the other hand, represents the sound of the spoken word, which in turn represents the person. Writing is therefore one step further removed from the child's experience. Moreover, the relationship between a picture of Mommy and Mommy herself is immediately obvious — one resembles the other. But the letters *M-O-M-M-Y* bear only a symbolic relationship to the person they represent. It takes learning for the youngster to grasp the notion that writing the word and drawing the picture express the very same idea.

When a toddler's random scribbles begin to give way to recognizable writing and drawing, she is beginning to make the distinction between these two paper-and-pencil activities. Even if she still speaks of "drawing" letters or "writing" a picture, she perceives that there is a difference. At first, she freely incorporates the new alphabet shapes she is learning into her drawings, along with many other shapes, as in the drawing below. Very soon, however, the special significance of the characters of writing becomes clear in the child's mind. Then the two elements — written and drawn — although still commonly combined on the page, begin to work together in ways that are increasingly sophisticated.

Your child may show her growing sophistication by signing her pictures, then writing one-word captions or labels for the drawings. Later, longer descriptions or messages may begin to appear. A child at this stage will usually draw the picture first, then cram the words anywhere she finds room on the page. Often she will not write from left to right and not necessarily from top to bottom. She may also break words arbitrarily, making small groups of letters that fit around the drawing. Only when her writing and drawing skills mature does she begin to plan pictures with space set aside for the writing. At that stage, she is learning how words and pictures can support each other and convey a more complete message than either one can alone.

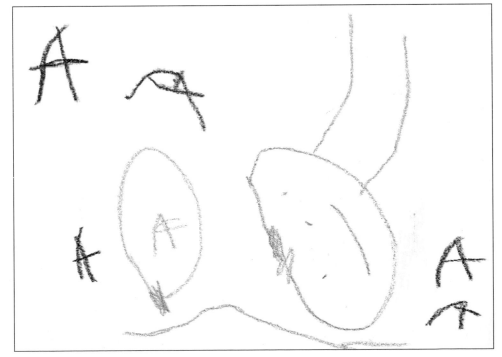

*The child who drew this picture knows how to form at least one letter but still makes no distinction between writing and drawing. The repeated "A's" do not represent a signature or any other message. The young artist uses these letters, like the circle and the human face, purely as pictorial elements in his drawing.*

GIRAFFE
AMA
WDA
FROM
to
AdAM

This drawing and its written message show a clear understanding of the difference between making pictures and writing. Although the five-year-old artist still does not write from top to bottom, she has labeled her drawing as a giraffe and inscribed it to read, ungarbled: "To Adam from Amanda." Clearly, the child did her drawing first, then added the writing wherever it would fit.

On this wish list for his sixth birthday, a child establishes a sophisticated relationship between the drawings and the writing. The pictures and words explain what he hopes to get. The presents he asks for, spelled more or less phonetically, are a calculator, spaceship, backpack, and Teddy bear, and three brand-name items: Inhumanoid, Voltron, and Wite-Out for making corrections.

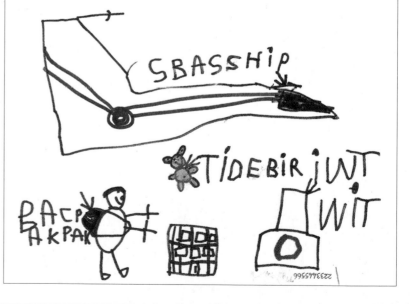

This drawing shows advanced storytelling ability, using a combination of words and pictures. The four-and-a-half-year-old child has learned the comic-strip convention of enclosing spoken words in balloons. Her tableau portrays a mother bird, with a worm dangling from her beak, greeting baby birds as they hatch out of their shells. The father says "No" to another bird, who is not a family member. The intruder says "O" and flies away.

# 3 Planting the Seeds

There is no magic formula for helping your child learn to read and write — only the magic in the time you spend with him. Whether you read the Sunday comics together, as the father and son are doing in the picture at the right, or take him shopping with you and let him pick items from the shelf, your youngster learns by being with you and by modeling his interests after yours.

By the time a child enters school, he has already acquired most of the skills needed for reading and writing. From listening and talking to you, he has learned how to communicate. By observing you read and write in your daily tasks and in your leisure moments, he has discovered that these are important and enjoyable activities. And by being included in family routines and outings, he has gained the background knowledge of people, places, and things that is so essential to reading development.

But before a child can learn to read and write, he also needs to believe in his ability to succeed. Unfortunately, some parents may unwittingly undermine their youngster's self-confidence by pushing him to read before he is ready, or just as bad, turn him off completely by changing what might be a pleasure into work. The pages that follow suggest entertaining activities that will foster your child's early interest in reading and writing without creating stress. It remains only for you to provide the relaxed, comfortable environment that will encourage him to experiment with and relish the process of learning.

# Your Child's Most Important Teacher

You have a major role to play in stimulating your child's interest in reading and writing. But it is a subtle one, requiring that you take a gentle and natural approach. Research has shown again and again that a child's ability to read depends much more on her early home environment than it does on the type of preschool program she attends or the size of her class once she enters elementary school.

When you take your young one to the local museum or zoo, you are helping her — perhaps without your even knowing it — build the self-confidence, experience, and concepts she will need to learn to read and write. Experts say it is not so much the type of activity that is important, but the way in which caring mothers and fathers interact with their children that makes the difference. Children who grow up in loving homes where parents spend time with them, go places with them, read aloud to them, help them pursue topics that they are interested in, engage them in conversation, and answer their questions have a big advantage when it comes to learning to read and write.

**Learning begins at home**

Each day is rife with possibilities for developing skills. You might let your youngster open the mail for you. Perhaps one of the envelopes will contain a batch of coupons. Encourage her to sort through them and find the pictures of the household items you normally buy. Another envelope might offer a treasure of wildlife stickers. Have her separate them and paste them onto pieces of paper.

Such an activity suits the kind of informal learning that is your young one's natural style. Far from feeling pressured to perform, as she might in a classroom, shc is likcly to bc completely relaxed. Because you made it all seem a game, she thoroughly enjoys it. That she also learned from it is almost incidental, but the accumulation of such small moments can make your youngster ready and eager to read and write once she enters school.

**Parents as examples**

You and your spouse are your child's models for reading and writing. The more you read and write in his presence, the more he will want to do so himself.

Avail yourself of every chance you get to demonstrate to your youngster the value and meaning of print. You might allow him to help you with activities that depend upon written instructions, such as baking a cake or assembling a toy. Perhaps you have just bought him a tricycle. After letting him experiment with putting it together, show him how much easier the task is when the instructions for assembly are followed.

Make your child aware of your interests and indicate how print lets you read about them. Take pains to encourage his own interests. On a trip to the library, help him pick out books that answer his many questions, say, about how hot the sun is and what it is like to be an astronaut and read them together to discover the answers. He is bound to notice how absorbed you get in reading a book or the newspaper, and he is likely to conclude that reading is an important activity.

Part of the appeal of reading for your youngster comes not only in imitating what you do, but in sharing what you do. Involving him in your conversation about the news on the front page of the newspaper or taking a moment to explain in simple terms the subject of the book you are currently reading helps him become aware of the magic of print.

Unfortunately, in today's busy world, many activities compete with reading — work, sports, television, and shopping, to name just a few. Keep in mind that how you divide up and spend your free moments is a more accurate indicator of what is important to you than what you tell your child. Make sure to set aside time for your own reading. Parents who manage to read for pleasure, despite their schedules, and whose homes are full of books, magazines, and newspapers convey to their children the idea that reading is a worthwhile pursuit.

Parents will be interested to learn that a youngster's slightly older brothers and sisters — or some other more experienced child she looks up to — can be of great help in preparing a preschooler to read. And why not? Children pick up just about everything else from their siblings.

*The boy pictured here is modeling his behavior after his mother's. Children who see their parents enjoying books learn early to appreciate the pleasures of reading.*

Having recently been through the whole thing herself, an older sister may instinctively know better how to go about the process of learning to read than the parents do. She is likely to have a stronger grip on what is interesting and important to a young beginning reader; adults who are long past this early stage in reading may wrongly identify what is simple or what is difficult. And an older sister is likely to be even more empathetic and helpful if she herself has experienced some difficulty or frustration at an earlier time, which she can still clearly remember. Moreover, it can be highly rewarding for the tutor, who feels very mature and wise and eager to learn even more in order to keep ahead of a younger sibling.

**Gender differences**

Most parents have come a long way from blindly accepting the rigid sexual stereotypes of the not-so-distant past. Yet even some of the most supportive parents continue to treat boys and girls differently in numerous subtle ways that may affect early reading ability. Girls are still encouraged to help their mothers in cooking, sorting laundry, and doing other household chores that provide informal opportunities for learning about reading and writing. From as young as the age of two, girls typically play with dolls, games, paints, and crayons, which encourage skills they will use in reading and writing. Boys, on the other hand, generally are led to vent their considerable physical energies in playing with blocks, toy vehicles, and active sports, which naturally limits the time for word games, puzzles, and other activities that enhance reading and writing skills. In a study of preschool play, researchers found that children who typically played with dolls and games scored higher in vocabulary testing, while those who played with blocks and toy vehicles scored higher on visual-spatial tasks.

Indeed, by the time children enter elementary school, many of those placed in the highest reading groups are girls, and their superiority continues until about the sixth grade, at which point the boys begin to catch up — at least in the United States and Canada. It is interesting to note that in two other English-speaking countries — Great Britain and Nigeria — the differences are exactly reversed; boys are by far the superior readers at an early age. Why? One possible explanation is that reading for boys is accorded a higher priority in those countries than it is in North America. All of this is a strong argument for the idea that cultural environment is a more likely cause of reading disparities between the sexes than any innate difference in early learning ability. ❖

# Benefits of Talking and Listening

Your child's oral language development depends on how — and how much — you talk to her during her early years. Studies have shown that children become articulate when parents enjoy conversing with them, refrain from constantly correcting their errors, and encourage them to play with language by initiating activities such as rhyming and storytelling. Keep in mind that the more opportunities your child has to talk, the more proficient she will become — and the bigger her vocabulary will be.

**Communicating fully with your child**

From the time he is born, your baby will enjoy having you talk and sing to him while cuddling in your arms. The close physical contact in these early exchanges not only builds his sense of security; it also brings out his innate desire to communicate. As you go through the daily routine of bathing, dressing, and feeding your baby, describe to him what you are doing. Though he will not understand the words, you will probably notice that he is listening closely to what you say, especially if you speak in an animated and happy voice.

When he begins babbling, wait until he finishes and then imitate the sounds he makes. By responding this way, you are treating him as a conversational partner long before he learns to speak. Encourage him to look at you as you speak so that he can see how your lips move to make different sounds. He will love your baby talk, but once he is beyond infancy, try to use correct names for objects. If you continue to use baby talk, you will only be reinforcing your child's immature speech patterns.

Between the ages of one and two, a youngster learns to communicate by using single words to express whole sentences. When your child stands at the door, saying, "Open," he is clearly indicating that he wants to go out. Picking up and expanding on his verbal clue, you

*A parent like this, who listens attentively to what her daughter has to say and asks questions to encourage her to talk, stimulates the development of language skills necessary for reading. Mealtimes often provide a relaxed atmosphere for such active listening.*

might respond: "Would you like to go out? Let me open the door for you. It's a beautiful day outside. You won't even need your jacket." Language experts call this type of response scaffolding because, in essence, you are providing the support for your child's language growth. The more support you give, the faster he will develop a wide vocabulary and the ability to use complex sentences. But keep in mind that it is also important to remove the support gradually as he gains competence. This prompts him to advance toward the next level of skills.

Once children have learned to express themselves, they rarely need encouragement to talk. Indeed, they are liable to gab incessantly and ask questions about everything: "Which is bigger, a giraffe or an elephant?" "How old will I be when you're a hundred?" "How long does it take to count to a billion?" Accustomed to the constant barrage of questions, parents sometimes answer them offhandedly, failing to recognize their significance. Try to remain patient; with the question about which animal is bigger, for instance, the child is forming a mental framework for classifying animals according to size.

**Encouraging your child to speak**

When your child speaks, try to be an active listener. This means not only paraphrasing what she says to show her you understand, but relating her comments to experiences she has had and helping her use logic to find answers to her questions. Your responsiveness will enhance her language skills and increase her background knowledge, which is important in reading.

Mealtimes offer one of the best opportunities for family conversations. To get your child talking, ask her questions about her day. Try to phrase your questions so that she will have to respond with more than one-word answers. For instance, instead of asking, "How was school today?" you might say, "Friday is show-and-tell day isn't it? What did everyone bring to share?"

Studies have also shown that children learn language more quickly when their parents talk to them, not at them, and react to what they say, rather than to how they say it. Constantly correcting your child's mistakes will only discourage her from talking. Nor is smiling or laughing at your youngster's errors, no matter how charming they are, a good idea. This will inhibit her willingness to experiment with language. Instead, you might try repeating or paraphrasing your child's statement as a way of correcting her. For instance, if she says, "Remember I telled you I want a drink," you might answer, "Yes, I do remember you told me you want a drink, and I'm going to get you one." By comparing her own speech with yours, she will correct herself over time. ⋱

# A World of Opportunity

Grownups take reading and writing so much for granted that they are not always conscious of how often these basic skills come into play in daily life. You may not have read a book or a newspaper on a particular day, but did you check the paper for the weather forecast or the television listings, consult a recipe, or look up a number in the phone book? Did you open your mail, jot down a note, or make a shopping list?

Simply including your youngster in these activities will turn them into valuable learning occasions. The key is not to attempt a formal lesson — which could be tedious both for you and your little one. If your child senses that you are intent on teaching him, he may lose interest quickly. But if you keep the emphasis on the fun and companionship of doing something together, you will see how quickly he develops a desire to learn language skills. And as he advances, you will find any number of useful ways to include his newfound abilities in the family's day-to-day life.

Cooking offers numerous fine learning opportunities for you and your youngster. He will love to help you measure and pour out the ingredients for pancake batter, which he can then enthusiastically stir. Be sure to show him the names on the package, milk container, and other items and to explain the marks on the measuring cup. Recipes, of course, are chockablock with combinations of words and numbers; point to each step while reading it aloud, so he will realize the importance of following written directions in sequence. Recipes often are a child's first introduction to abbreviations, and he will be intrigued when you tell him what they mean. As always, be prepared for mistakes. Inevitably, your small helper will spill something on the floor or wipe his gooey hands on his pants. Try not to become impatient; it will only discourage him from wanting to help you the next time.

Occasionally, you may want to join him in planning a special luncheon for a friend — or a treat for the family. If he seems to be a budding

*Helping his mother make pancakes, this youngster is learning an important lesson about written instructions while enjoying a grown-up activity.*

cook, you might consider buying him a children's cookbook, one that features menus for young people in easy-to-read print and pictures.

Although many parents dread having to control an active pre-schooler in a shopping cart, a trip to the supermarket can be an excellent way to acquire language skills. Before setting out, have your child help you make a grocery list by writing or dictating the names of some favorite foods. At the store, turn your shopping into a treasure hunt. As you wheel your cart through the cereal section, ask him to tell you when he sees the kind on your list. Almost all youngsters can recognize the package of the cereal they like best, even though they may be too young to read.

Children seem to be entranced by coupons, perhaps because they are so colorful and such fun to cut out of newspapers or magazines. Go through the pages with your youngster, helping him find items on your list and reading how much you will save. If you let him hold the coupons while you shop, he can use them as visual clues in his search for the items you want. Some parents allow their young readers to keep the money saved with coupons as a reward for their efforts.

**The daily routine**     Much of your youngster's daily routine, from morning to bed-time, lends itself to learning about the printed word. At break-fast, you can write out a menu that offers her simple choices. Under drinks, you might list apple juice or orange juice in addition to her regular milk. Under cereal, you might write down whatever brands you happen to have on hand. And an egg could be boiled, fried, or scrambled. While falling in with the make-believe of playing restaurant, she will also be learning about the function of print.

You can reinforce your child's growing eagerness to learn about language by posting a large planning calendar on a wall where she can easily see it. She will look forward to checking the calendar with you each day to see what events or activities have been scheduled. Gradually, she will become familiar with the days of the week and the months of the year, while at the same time gaining an appreciation for the importance of reading and writing in organizing one's life. A wall chart can help in other ways, as well. Many children are more willing to perform their chores, such as dressing themselves or brushing their teeth, if you make a chart that rewards them with a check mark or a sticker for a job well done. Even if the chart includes three or four different categories, your youngster will soon be able to recognize each one.

**Finding time to read**

How often have you had to wait with your youngster at a doctor's or a dentist's office, a restaurant, or any number of other places? Life sometimes seems to be one great waiting game, but you can make the time count for your preschooler by getting in the habit of taking along a storybook wherever you go. Auto travel, in particular, can be subject to numerous delays, and is generally boring. You will find it useful to keep a variety of books in the family car and to arm yourself with some interesting language-related games *(pages 86-89)*.

It is important to set aside a regular time each day for reading so that your youngster will come to look forward to it as part of his daily routine. Many parents prefer to have storytime just before bedtime because it helps their child unwind from his busy day; a relaxing story at this quiet time of day will help him go to sleep feeling loved and secure. As he grows older, you may wish to extend storytime by allowing him to look at a book by himself in bed for fifteen or twenty minutes before turning out the light. This will encourage him to think of himself as a reader.

Actually, any time can and should be storytime. All youngsters like being read to, and the spontaneous session that comes as a reward for good behavior or just because you and your young one are both ready for it will be doubly valuable and enjoyable.

**Looking for chances to write**

Besides reading together, try to find time to encourage your child's writing activities. When you are writing, have her sit next to you so she can see your pen moving across the paper from left to right. Explain what you are writing, such as a letter to Grandma, and ask if she has anything she would like to add. If she

*As a treat, this boy was allowed to keep his book in bed with him after his father had finished reading to him. Like his Teddy bear, books are becoming beloved companions.*

*This little girl is learning firsthand the meaning of writing as she pens a letter to Grandma, mails it (below), and receives and opens a card from Grandma in response (opposite). Writing to a relative fosters an understanding of writing as a means of communicating with someone far away.*

is old enough to write the words by herself, have her do so, no matter how messy the results may be. If writing her name is all she can manage, have her tell you what she wishes to say and then let her sign the letter herself.

Once the letter is finished, she will feel very grown-up if she is able to mail it herself. You might also consider asking relatives or friends to send postcards and letters to your youngster. Children love to receive mail, and a letter addressed especially to your child is usually all the encouragement she will need to write back. You might also wish to subscribe in her name to a children's magazine. Before you do, however, it is a good idea to borrow copies of several different magazines from the library to help you pick out the one that is best suited to her age and interests.

Many youngsters enjoy keeping a journal, and it can be a wonderful activity long before she masters conventional writing. Your youngster's journal can be a place for her to scribble or draw or dictate to you her thoughts about subjects that interest her. Do not worry about how the beginner's writing looks or how she spells; at this stage, the activity itself is the important thing, and she will ask for your help if she wants it. As your little one's writing ability improves, look for ways she can put it to use. She will enjoy helping out, and giving her responsibilities she can easily handle will foster her sense of competence. Ask your child to make a list of emergency telephone numbers to tape near each phone. Or take advantage of a family get-together, such as Thanksgiving, to let her make place cards. You can dictate the spelling of the names or make a list for her to copy — or you can let her try *Grandma* and *Grandpa* on her very own.

You might also encourage her to

make and sign the valentines and birthday cards that she sends to friends and
relatives. When her birthday comes
around, let her make a guest list and write
the invitations, if she wishes. And when she
draws pictures, suggest that she sign them,
preferably in the upper left-hand corner, which will
reinforce her sense of where print begins on a page
and which way it goes.

**Being a "word detective"**

The world is filled with print, and you can encourage
your youngster's reading skills by asking him questions about
the signs and symbols everywhere. Appoint him to be a "word
detective" and to find familiar letters or words on signs. Most
youngsters, for instance, see the letters *S-T-O-P* in the familiar
context of a red octagon on a street corner and know immediately what the word means. Identifying printed words in context is
very exciting for your youngster. Although he may not yet be
able to identify a word out of context, he now begins to think of
himself as a reader in the same way that he does while looking at
a book before bedtime.

Another way to help your preschooler explore print is to label
his belongings and other objects around the house. Every youngster loves to see things named, and the activity will foster both
his writing skills and reading comprehension. Signs might range
from "Tommy's room" to "back door" or "exit" — a word that
seems to fascinate many children. You may have to write the
words first and let him trace or copy them. Once the signs are up,
the objects themselves will help him recognize the words, and
before long, he can try spelling them out for you.

**Making television a reading tool**

The impact that television has on children can be awesome —
just ask any mother who has heard her child demand a certain
brand of breakfast cereal or laundry detergent by piping its
catchy jingle. And too much TV has negative effects on reading
readiness in youngsters: Families who view a lot of television are generally not reading families; children who
spend hours upon hours before the tube often lack interest in reading or the concentration to develop reading
skills. What is more, the nervous and muscular systems of
small children seem to be adversely affected by prolonged TV
watching; those little heads cannot process the masses of information being dinned at them, and their bodies suffer from all that
sitting or lying around.

Yet properly regulated, TV can enhance your youngster's readiness to read by heightening interest in books and by strengthening vocabulary, word formation, rhyming, and spelling. Indeed, a number of popular children's shows are aimed specifically at preparing children for reading. And any suitable, well-conceived show will share a number of common elements with books, such as dialogue, character development, plot, and setting.

The first step, of course, is to place firm limits on the amount of time your child spends before the TV set: about an hour in any one day is usually enough; and your preschooler should not get into the habit of watching TV every single day. Naturally, you should pay close attention to the programs she watches.

In addition to such popular children's programs as "Sesame Street," "Reading Rainbow," and "Mr. Rogers' Neighborhood," be on the lookout for specials related to your child's growing interests. Nature programs, such as those put on by the National Geographic Society, appeal to most youngsters' love of animals and curiosity about the world. If you own a video cassette recorder, you might wish to scout out your library or video rental store for its children's offerings; most of them have collections that include animated versions of popular fairy tales and other well-known children's classics, such as Dr. Seuss stories and *Winnie the Pooh.*

*Although the youngster signaling "stop" has not yet learned to read, she can recognize the letters S-T-O-P in the familiar context of a red octagonal sign. For most children, learning to identify words by their context is the first step toward reading.*

Whenever possible, watch TV with your child so that you can answer her questions as they arise and follow up subjects in which she shows a particular interest. If she is intrigued by a program about polar bears, you might find books to share with her about how polar bears find food and stay warm in the Arctic winters. Or you might use her interest as a steppingstone to explore how animals are camouflaged to blend in with their environment. There are many entryways from television into the world of books. In fact, that favorite program "Sesame Street" has led to a series of books that children love to read, featuring such characters as the Cookie Monster, Oscar the Grouch, Ernie and Bert, and Big Bird.

## Making the Most of Going Places Together

The time you spend driving with your youngster in the family car can be used to foster his language skills. But be sure to pick activities that emphasize fun; you do not want to make him feel that you are instructing him. Here are some for you to try:

- Point out road signs, such as "Yield" and "No Passing," and explain to your child what they mean.
- Take turns making up nonsense verse, such as, "I was walking down the street and I saw a SKUNK/And what did he have but an alligator TRUNK. /It looked kind of small, I think it must have SHRUNK . . . "
- Ask him to identify landmarks and street signs along the route and to navigate the trip home; a handmade map of the route might add to the adventure.
- Encourage him to look at road signs and billboards to find certain letters of the alphabet or those of his name. You may want to keep score by giving him one point for each letter he finds and playing till he reaches ten or twenty points.
- For longer trips, bring along books and a cassette player and tapes that make it possible for your child to follow the pictures in a book while the narrator tells the story.
- Tell him a story or ask him to tell you one. If you are stuck for ideas, try relating the story to the drive you are taking. For instance, you might begin, "A little boy whose name was Tommy was riding with his mother in their car one day when all at once a tiny, tiny spaceship landed right on the car's roof . . . "

**Tips for working parents**

If you work outside the home, you may find it hard to include your child in errands and housekeeping tasks; it is often more convenient to do such chores at lunchtime, on the way home, or in the evening. Nonetheless, there are still plenty of opportunities to prepare your child for reading and writing. Try to keep books and writing materials on hand in the kitchen to busy your child while you prepare meals. Many youngsters enjoy playing with the magnetic letters that stick to a refrigerator, or they are happy to sit near you and color or scribble. If it is impractical to involve him in cooking at the moment, you can build language ability by chatting with him or by playing word games.

You can do more of the same in the morning while driving to the day-care center. And it is fun for your child if you leave messages for him to find in his lunch box. Many children will quickly learn to recognize such simple sentences as "I love you" or "I miss you," and will grin with pleasure when they read them.

Encourage your baby-sitter or day-care provider to include activities that promote reading and writing *(pages 86-89)*. Later, in conversing with your child about his day, you can learn about the types of activities he enjoys most and then do them together at home. Above all, no matter how pressed you are for time, make sure you read with your youngster every day. It will show him that you value reading and the time you spend with him more than any of the other activities you could be doing. You are liable to find it so relaxing and enjoyable that you will look forward to it as greatly as your little one does. ❖

# Amassing Experience

As an adult, you derive meaning not only from the words you read on the page, but also from your previous experience with the subject. This knowledge often enables you to predict what comes next; reading goes faster and is more enjoyable.

The same very much applies to your youngster; you can add to her delight and comprehension by exposing her to a wide range of experiences in the outside world — things that she will later be reading about. One study, for example, tested a number of second-graders on their knowledge of spiders, then asked them to read a passage about spiders; not surprisingly, the children who were already familiar with spiders scored higher in the reading-comprehension test.

This is not to suggest that you have to fill your house with spiders. But do expand your little one's horizons whenever you can. Most of it will come naturally. Plays, puppet shows, and museum exhibits geared for children are all good ways to build her fund of knowledge for reading; so is a visit to the local airport or fire station, or a short bus or train ride.

Youngsters learn best by becoming engaged in an activity, particularly when a number of senses are brought into play. At a petting zoo, for instance, a child not only sees a goat, she touches its soft coat, hears its bleat, and smells its distinctive barnyard odor. And if you and your three-year-old can visit a farm where she can pick apples, she will learn a lot about where her food comes from; otherwise, she might think it all just comes from the grocery store.

**Turning an outing into an adventure** As you plan an outing, think how you can heighten the experience for your child. One good way to stimulate her interest is to read to her in advance about what she is going to see and hear and smell and touch. And you will of course want to follow up afterward, when your youngster is bound to have lots of questions. If you can manage to respond to the questions by reading the information to her, so much the better. One of the most important lessons you can get across is that reading rewards people with answers to questions about the world.

While you and your young one are on the excursion, try to make it more of an adventure by bringing along tools for you both to use. A hike in the woods will be more fun and more meaningful if you carry a magnifying glass with which to examine the treasures you find along the way, such as leaves and acorns, or perhaps a worm. You might take your camera and snap some pictures that will reinforce her memories of the experience. The photos will also make a fine scrapbook; for captions,

she can dictate to you her impressions of what she saw. Ask questions to draw out her thoughts and help her relate the experience to other events in her life.

When a trip to your local museum sparks an interest in a particular subject, such as dinosaurs, accompany your youngster to the library to find books on prehistoric animals. At home, you can add other activities such as drawing pictures of dinosaurs, and then labeling them and sorting them into categories, such as meat-eaters or plant-eaters. Or you might consider buying your child a small bag of plastic dinosaurs to play with in the bathtub. If she seems fascinated by the idea of digging for fossils, give her a shovel and turn her loose in the sandbox or a corner of the backyard in a game of make-believe. You might enhance the game by burying small objects for her to discover.

**Social and community events**

By the time she is two, your youngster may be ready to join a weekly play group, have an occasional play-date with a friend, or visit a nearby playground — all activities that will help develop language skills. Playgrounds provide opportunities to interact on neutral territory with other children. Though arguments are inevitable, try to intervene as little as possible. Letting children work out their problems by themselves encourages their language abilities and builds self-reliance. Many youngsters enjoy carrying on a conversation with older children and adults. You may be surprised how grown-up your youngster sounds when she is talking to an adult other than yourself. This shows her growing awareness that words should be chosen to suit both the audience and the occasion.

Another way to help build your child's language skills is to involve her in library story hours for preschoolers *(pages 72-73)* and other literary activities in your neighborhood. Many schools have book fairs featuring children's authors, and community organizations often sponsor guest appearances by local storytellers. ❖

*While a storyteller reads to two-year-olds, the youngsters are free not only to walk about, but to come closer for a better view of a picture, or to cuddle with their mothers.*

# The Library Treasure House

Do you remember your first trip to the public library as a child and how exciting it was to find there an Ali Baba's cave of books, all of them waiting for you to take home?

Today's library is an even more wondrous place, with reading programs designed to appeal to children as young as two. The best of these programs stimulate a toddler's interest in reading through special storytimes, in which child and parent alike participate. The parent's or caregiver's presence helps assuage any anxieties the youngster might have about strange places and new faces and also provides the kind of direct involvement that enhances the experience.

Typically, story-hour programs are held weekly, with the participants enrolled in advance. Since two-year-olds are very active, staying seated is hard for them. The storyteller takes this into account and lets them move about while she reads aloud or invites questions. The library thus becomes a friendly place to them — even one to explore.

So that the experience will be consistently lively, story hour often includes other broadening activities: songs and marching to help develop a sense of rhythm and movement; puppet shows and creative dramatics to nourish new skills in make-believe; seed plantings and animal studies to enlarge a sense of the natural world.

As always, librarians stand ready and willing to help you find appropriate books for your youngster, whatever his age, and to offer ideas for home projects that will enhance his pleasure in books of all kinds and increase his store of background knowledge. And as a reflection of today's world, libraries now offer records, audiocassettes, and videotapes designed to stimulate your child's interest in stories still further.

*Here storytelling is combined with other activities, including finger-play songs (left) and crafts (above). Some are timed to the seasons, as in spring when children color paper flowers and plant seeds in paper cups to take home.*

Story hour stimulates children to want books. A display arranged on the floor by the storyteller and related to the day's read-aloud theme entices one prospective borrower (top left). Other youngsters enjoy supervised browsing in the child-high stacks of the children's section (above). At left, a girl hands her storybooks to the librarian for check-out on her mother's library card, while another youngster heads proudly home with a prized selection.

# Encouraging an Interest in Print

Before your youngster can become literate, he must grasp the concept that reading and writing are powerful tools of communication. This is why it is so important to plan daily activities that allow your youngster to see how society revolves around reading and writing, and to include him in ways that allow him to experiment with these marvelous inventions. But there is much more you can do to stimulate his growing fascination with the wonderfully exciting world of print. This section focuses on practical methods you can use to bathe, as it were, your little one in language.

As you work with your youngster, your goal is to foster his image of himself as a reader and writer so that he will eventually come to explore books and written language on his own. The best way to accomplish this is to provide him with a generous supply of reading and writing materials, plenty of ideas at first, lots of encouragement — and a gentle helping hand whenever he asks you for it.

**Individual learning styles**

Let yourself be guided by your youngster's interests. Every child is different, and the best clues to your small one's particular style of learning are the activities that she initiates herself. Some children respond enthusiastically to word games, such as riddles and rhymes; others like nothing better than to sit at the kitchen table and copy letters off the back of a cereal box or something else with print on it. But whatever appeals to her, keep in mind that all small children like to be busy — so be prepared to offer suggestions that you know will capture her interest when she finishes one project and asks: "Mommy, what's there to do next?"

Do not be afraid to initiate something new every once in a while. Children sometimes need to be presented with a challenge in order to expand their play. Whatever you do, make sure that what you suggest is suitable to your youngster's age and ability level. A youngster of two years may delight in listening while you recite a favorite nursery rhyme, while a three-year-old will take greater pleasure in having you pause just be-

*"Look, Mom, it's an A, just like in Adam!" This youngster's exclamation over discovering a letter from his name in a bowl of alphabet soup is typical of the excitement children feel when they begin to recognize letters. Providing as much print as possible in a child's environment will stimulate his curiosity about writing.*

fore the last word so that she can fill in the missing word herself.

You may wonder how you will know when your youngster is ready for more advanced word play. Generally, the questions that she asks will give you an indication. For example, once she discovers that the letters of the alphabet have distinctive characteristics — which usually happens somewhere between the ages of three and four — she will be eager to practice making them and will begin asking all sorts of questions, such as, "How do you make a *C?*"

You can avoid the mistake of overteaching, or going beyond your child's interest and ability level, by limiting your answers to the specific information she seeks. Here, for example, you should show her how to make a *C.* But do not assume that just because she is eager to learn how a letter is formed that she is ready to associate it with a particular sound; you might casually direct her attention to some familiar words that begin with *C,* but it would be inappropriate at this stage to ask her to come up with them. She will let you know when she is ready for that. One day she might suddenly make the delighted observation: "Hey, Mommy, *dog* and *Dad* start with the same sound!" Now would be the right time for you to follow up by asking her what other words start with that letter or that sound. Once she has an idea of how letters and sound correspond, she might ask, "Mommy, how do you spell *happy?*" Tell her and write it out if she asks you to. She is clearly making giant strides in language.

**Building more supports**

Just as you provided support, or scaffolding, for your youngster's early oral efforts by filling in the words he did not know, you should now stand ready to buttress his development as a reader and writer. Secure in the knowledge that he can call on you for help, he will be more willing to experiment with his new skills and take chances.

When your youngster first becomes interested in written language, for example, he will be happy just to scribble, making great free-wheeling circles and curves and bold lines. By letting him know that you accept his scribble writing as the real thing, you will be encouraging him to continue doing it — and to keep on making progress. Later, when he is keen to practice more conventional writing — usually between the ages of four and five — he may want to try copying your writing. Then, in the next stage, he may begin composing his own sentences, using spellings that are his own invention. If at any point he should ask for your help in spelling or in suggesting an idea to

# An Expert's View

## The Dangers of Pushing a Child

Many of us involved in early childhood education are alarmed at the recent trend toward using formal methods to teach youngsters to read at an early age. All across the country, academic programs devised for school-age children are now being applied to preschoolers as well. Four-year-olds are bringing home workbooks and papers once reserved for first-graders. And a growing number of how-to books for parents advocate the teaching of reading and math to infants.

Apart from a lack of evidence that early formal instruction has any lasting benefits for children, such inappropriate teaching methods may actually have a negative effect on a youngster's motivation, intellectual growth, and self-esteem. For the growing number of preschoolers exposed to this miseducation, there is a real danger of burnout once they reach elementary school.

Unfortunately, the new emphasis on early education too often reflects the priorities of adults rather than the needs of children. The result has been a tendency to ignore one of the basic understandings about early childhood — that young children learn differently from older children and adults. Young children learn by trial and error — by actively exploring and manipulating concrete materials, such as balancing a stack of blocks or putting together a puzzle. In doing so, they construct mental categories and generalizations that form the basis for their intellectual growth. Their natural curiosity and desire to make sense of their world will lead them spontaneously to activities that develop essential cognitive skills. Children beginning to learn quantity concepts, for instance, will count everything in sight.

When a child is forced to spend time on rote memorization and drill, rather than on activities he himself initiates, he may lose his desire to learn. And if his parents give the impression that his self-directed activities are not as worthwhile as the "educational" ones they have chosen, his initiative may give way to a sense of guilt.

Formal instruction also can be harmful to youngsters by inculcating in them erroneous notions of what is correct and what is incorrect. Workbooks and papers that put all their emphasis on giving the right answer inhibit a child's willingness to experiment and make mistakes. His self-worth then becomes dependent on adult approval rather than on his own feelings of mastery of the tasks he has chosen.

For all these reasons, teaching four-year-olds as though they were seven-year-olds puts them under too much pressure. Pediatricians report seeing preschoolers with such stress-related symptoms as headaches and stomachaches. In my own studies, I have observed youngsters who were driven to read by their parents exhibit apathy and withdrawal — classic symptoms of burnout.

While it is true that some children teach themselves to read before entering school, other children have been prodded into reading by ambitious parents who need to bolster their own egos through the accomplishments of their child. Regrettably, the advantages of early instruction are likely to be short-lived for the precocious reader who is not self-taught. Experience shows that children who are introduced to reading and writing at a later developmental stage take less time to acquire such skills and are more spontaneous and enthusiastic readers at adolescence than those forced to read earlier.

Many parents feel compelled to push their children into early education for another reason. There has been a large increase in the number of single-parent households and mothers entering the work force. But these changes in our society have not been accompanied by an adequate provision for child care. Working parents, under pressure to find all-day care facilities, may convince themselves that their youngster is mature enough to handle an accelerated program that keeps him in school until their own workday is over.

The welter of facts brought into the home via television and computers has given many young children a pseudosophistication that contributes to the misconception that they are ready for formal reading instruction. While it is true that today's youngsters have access to more information than previous generations, there is no evidence that this exposure to technology accelerates their development in any way. Knowing about a subject is not the same as understanding that subject. Moreover, learning to decode written symbols does not automatically lead to comprehension of the material decoded. More generally, children who watch television a great deal become accustomed to gaining information pictorially, and this makes them reluctant to put in the effort it takes to read.

Finally, I want to make it clear that I am not automatically opposed to creative school programs for four-year-olds, or to all-day kindergartens that enhance youngsters' knowledge and experience of the world and themselves. Certainly, with 50 percent of mothers of preschoolers now in the work force, there is a real need for such programs. What I am saying is that to be of real service to parents and to children, the programs must be based on sound principles of early childhood education. In other words, they need to be geared to the modes of learning of young children and not function as downward extensions of elementary education.

*— David Elkind, Ph.D.*
*Professor of Child Study and Resident Scholar*
*Lincoln Filene Center, Tufts University*

get him started, by all means give it to him. But do not push.

As your youngster grows older and gains competence, you will probably want to modify the sort of help you provide. Once a task becomes easy for him, you might gently try to make it just a bit more challenging. When he becomes familiar enough with letters to begin attempts at spelling, print out the letters he asks for in his word building. As he gets more adept at making letters, he might enjoy having you call out letters for him to write from memory — a much more advanced task.

Throughout, allow your child to take the lead and try not to press ahead too fast. He might point to *dog,* and ask: "What does that word say?" You can simply tell him, without going overboard in your answer. Do not respond by insisting that he sound out the word *dog* himself, or by delivering a five-minute lecture on the short *o* vowel sound. Later, when your youngster has learned something about the way letters and sounds correspond, you might assist him in identifying the first and last letters of a word. At this point, he might combine them and figure out the *o* for himself.

**Ways to explore storybooks**

When your child begins to adopt favorite storybooks, you might occasionally ask him to "read" you a story — one that he is familiar with and that has lots of repetition. He will proudly think of himself as a reader, even though he has not yet acquired all the skills. As he proceeds, you will be able to see how well he understands the function of print. If his eyes focus on the illustrations, and he gives a disjointed account of them, he is still in the early stages of print awareness and thinks that reading involves interpreting the pictures.

You can help foster his awareness of letters and words by pointing to the text as you read to him. If he finds this too distracting, try a more subtle approach: When you open the book, ask him to show you where you should begin. Or, when he inadvertently covers up the print with his hand or tries to turn the page before you are finished reading, explain to him that you need to see the words in order to know what is happening in the story.

When reading aloud to your youngster, stop frequently to ask questions or add information that will help him understand the text. You should always try to relate it to his own experience. While reading "The Three Little Pigs," for example, you might say, "This little pig's house is made of bricks, just like our house. Why do you suppose bricks are better than straw for building a house?" Or, "What do you think the wolf meant by 'I'll huff and

# Aa Bb Cc Dd Ee Ff

puff?' " Questions such as, "What's another word for tired?" also nurture his understanding of the meaning of *word*.

As time goes by, his way of reading a story from memory will begin to sound like a written text, indicating his growing awareness of the differences between spoken and written language. Do not discourage him by giving him the impression that you consider his way of reading "just pretend." And, even more important, do not yield to the temptation to have him try sounding out actual letters or words. Your goal should be simply to encourage his interest in print, not to teach him how to read — not right now.

Soon he may point to familiar letters and begin associating them with their sounds or even begin identifying simple words, such as *no* and *go.* At this point he may also show an interest in print mapping: that exercise in which a youngster tries to match letters and words on the page with their spoken equivalents. If he asks for your help in this, be prepared to give it to him generously. But when you sense that he is losing interest, be quick to stop and move on to something else. And remember — just by reading to him often and giving him the freedom to explore print on his own, you are helping him understand how it works.

**The importance of scribbling**

Encouraging your child's early scribbling will help her grasp what writing is all about — communication. Most often, you need only supply your little one with paper and crayons or markers, and let her go at it. Youngsters also love to scribble in the sand with a stick or on a chalkboard, and finger paints are a great favorite. You can make your own edible finger paint by combining one egg yolk, two tablespoons of water, and a few drops of food coloring. Mix up some colors, lay out a large piece of paper on the floor or tape it to a wall, and stand back. Finger painting will be satisfyingly messy for her. But if it is too untidy for you, you might offer her the bathtub finger paints that come in the form of tubes of soap.

In her earliest efforts, your youngster is not really expressing a thought or drawing distinguishable pictures. She is simply enjoying her newfound power to make marks on a blank surface. Be sure to give her plenty of encouragement as you watch her at

*With homemade alphabet strips like these, you can encourage your child to use both uppercase and lowercase letters, a practice advisable for even the youngest writers. Post them near the area where he usually does his play writing.*

# Nn Oo Pp Qq Rr Ss Tt

work. Try to concentrate your comments on the act of writing rather than on the product. Tracing over your child's swirls with your finger, you might say, "Wow, I like the way you made those curvy lines," rather than "That's a very nice picture. What is it supposed to be?"

A good way to help your child progress from scribble writing to conventional writing is to give her opportunities to watch you write. Letting her sit beside you while you write a letter, for example, will spark her interest and encourage her to pay attention. By watching you, she will notice that most letters are made from the top down and have certain characteristics that occur over and over again.

When your youngster's scribbles begin to resemble actual letters, resist the temptation to press ahead and attempt to teach her real letters at this point. As with reading, a satisfactory first goal is to encourage her to think of herself as a budding writer. Do not focus attention on her shortcomings. Expecting her to learn the correct way to hold a pencil or to form letters before she is ready will only undermine her confidence and natural enthusiasm. Generally, as their muscles mature — between the ages of three and four — children begin to switch from gripping a pencil with their fist to holding it with their fingers, without any parental tutoring.

**Learning the alphabet**

When children begin to recognize the letters of the alphabet, usually between the ages of two and a half and four, they are entering a stage the experts call letter awareness. Considering a youngster's natural curiosity, the phrase is something of an understatement. For once youngsters can identify a few letters, they begin to notice them everywhere — on packages, billboards, storefronts, even on toilets.

This is the perfect moment to post an alphabet chart, like the one shown below, on a wall near the spot where your preschooler does most of his writing. And now is the time to lavish him with materials, such as alphabet blocks, alphabet puzzles, and magnetic letters. Once he knows how a letter is formed, he will be happy to trace it or copy it repeatedly until he has learned to make it by himself.

In the process of copying, he will inevitably reverse some

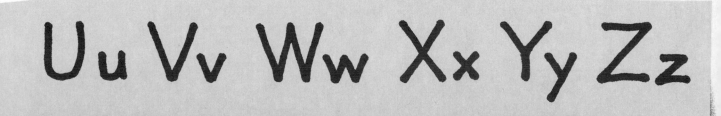

*While a young doctor writes out a prescription, her patient looks up from the magazines she has been reading in a make-believe waiting room. When children incorporate print into their play, they are beginning to understand its importance in their culture.*

letters *(page 51).* Do not fret. All youngsters progress at their own pace; they listen to their mind's own music. Just ignore the imperfections; they will disappear with time and experience.

As you have already discovered, the letters that make up your youngster's name will hold a special magic for her. Even before she recognizes all the letters of the alphabet, your little one will love to see her name in print and will be eager to practice writing it herself.

As you help her get started, be sure to say each letter aloud when you print it out and carefully describe how it is made. If her name begins with a *P,* you might say, "Start at the top and make a line that goes straight down, like this. Then go back to the top and make a curved line that goes out and then down and then back again until it meets the straight line, like this." It is a good idea to use both uppercase and lowercase letters since she will eventually have to learn to differentiate between them and how they are used.

Once she has learned to write her name, look for opportunities for her to practice her new skill. Aside from signing her name on drawings, messages, and letters, she can write her name on her books, her toys, or on a nameplate for her bedroom door. In some communities, a child is eligible to have her own library card when she can write her name — a wonderful reward for her progress.

**Playing with print**

From realizing that his own name consists of a number of letters, your youngster will gradually understand that all words are made up of letters. Just as he got the hang of spoken language by experimenting with sound, he will now exercise his fledgling writing skills. By offering praise — and support when he asks for it — you can help him advance rapidly.

Give him a little boost by encouraging him to make up stories, the more imaginative the better. Offer to write them down for him. Your youngster may love to tell stories but not be far enough along in his

*The youngster pictured here pretends to look up a number in an old phone book that her parents have given her. Props that develop familiarity with reading and writing as a form of play stimulate interest in print.*

perception of print to know that they can be written down. When he reaches that realization, he may welcome having you as his secretary, and when he sees his words written down on paper, he will probably become totally absorbed in them. At this point, the two of you may enjoy making a storybook together (page 82). Around the age of five, he will have achieved a good grasp of the process of writing. Now when he dictates to you, he will pace his speech to give you time to write it down. With your help in spelling, he may even be ready to try writing his stories himself.

Many five- and six-year-olds talk nonstop as they write and get so interested in talking that they lose track of their story line. You may want to help by reading his story back to him several times so that he can complete his train of thought. You may also have to remind him that it is important to leave spaces between words in his story and to arrange the words in the order they are spoken.

To whet his interest, set aside a special time regularly for both of you to write. You can help kindle his imagination by posing interesting questions. However, you should also reinforce the notion that writing is used for everyday tasks, as well. While you catch up with your own correspondence, you might suggest that he write a note to remind you that he has been invited to play at a friend's house next week.

The best opportunities for writing often arise spontaneously. Your youngster might suddenly interrupt your newspaper reading to tell you something so amusing or eloquent that you want to preserve it in written form. Delighted at having captured your attention, he may wind up telling you an entire story.

It is still far too early, of course, to expect him to distinguish all the letter sounds or to know that all English words must have at least one vowel. But you can still encourage him to spell words by writing the sounds he does know his own way. Using his own invented spelling, he might write, "I played baseball," something like this: "I pd bsbl."

**The writing game**  You will know that your preschooler has a solid grasp of the function of print when he begins to use writing in his play. This

*With adultlike concentration, a boy carefully writes down his mother's order for lunch — just as he has seen the waiter do it at a restaurant. His mother wisely realizes that using reading and writing in play is more educational than doing drills in workbooks.*

## The Pleasures of Making a Book

One of the best ways to spark your child's early interest in books is to help him make his own. Children love the planning, writing, coloring, cutting, and pasting involved in "publishing" a book. And both you and your youngster will derive a strong sense of accomplishment from the finished product — as long as you keep it simple.

For toddlers, books with a theme are an ideal way to start. Let your child go through an old magazine or catalogue with you and point to familiar items in a particular category, such as clothes or food. You will probably have to cut the pictures out, but he will want to help you paste them on the pages. Ask him to identify them one at a time as you print names underneath each. Construction paper or cardboard makes excellent pages; fasten the pages together with a stapler or by punching holes and tying them with thread or yarn.

For a more permanent book, try sewing together several sturdy plastic sandwich bags that have zipper-like closures. Line each bag with construction paper or cardboard and place a picture on each side. The beauty of the bags is that you can insert new pictures when your youngster's interests change —

photographs of dinosaurs, trucks, or baseball players, for example, instead of barnyard creatures.

A touch-and-feel book will delight most infants and toddlers. Their approach to learning is strictly hands-on at this stage, and such a book will give them free play. Your home is a treasure trove of fascinating items: Aluminum foil, sandpaper, and cotton balls are a few. Make the book even more interesting by including a few peekaboo pages, with flaps hiding magazine pictures — or perhaps snapshots of family and friends.

As your child grows, a story dictated by him to you will make a great manuscript for a book. He will feel even more like an author if his story is typed on a typewriter, or better still, on one of those seemingly magical machines, a computer. Encourage him to illustrate his story and to make a cover complete with title, author, and date. He may even want to write a dedication.

One five-year-old was having so much fun making a book with his mom that it went on for five chapters. At the end, his mother remarked, "You know, I think you might just be a writer one day." At which her son clasped the book to his chest and firmly announced, "I already am!"

usually occurs around the age of three. A youngster playing doctor, for instance, may ask you for a notepad and a pencil so that he can write out prescriptions for the medicine his patient needs. Or he may deputize himself as a policeman and issue a ticket for speeding, just as he saw happen on TV — or perhaps the last time you got caught.

You can encourage these advances in writing skills by suggesting other roles to play and by providing the necessary props, such as clothes for playing dress-up, old telephone books, magazines, and pencils and notepads. Young children love playing restaurant and taking orders for lunch or dinner, and they get a kick out of using a discarded phone book for make-believe calls. Older preschoolers may be ready to set up a lemonade stand complete with sign. Or they may want to form a club with written rules and a list of members. Playing school is another good activity; the children may not know exactly what happens in school, but the play gets them accustomed to the idea of formal learning.

When your child invites you into his play, you can suggest additional ways to incorporate print into the fun. For example, if he asks for your help in pushing together chairs to make a pretend train, bring him a pencil and notepad and say, "Here, I thought we might need these for making tickets for our passengers." He will appreciate the thought and may now ask you to print up a little money for them to spend.

**In praise of trying** When children are first learning to talk, most parents naturally — and wisely — focus on what their little ones are saying and ignore the pronunciation and grammatical errors. Alas, those same parents do not always show the same wisdom when it comes to print. For some reason, many adults expect their youngster to meet grown-up standards from the day she first picks up a crayon. Catch yourself before you say things like, "No, that's not the right way to hold it." And when you observe her happily making marks across a page, try not to ask, "What letter is that supposed to be?" Needless to say, such remarks will quickly discourage the most eager child.

When she comes to show you some writing she is proud of, resist the temptation to correct her spelling; do not point out that her writing meanders downhill or uphill. And steel yourself against the inevitable messes she will make as she experiments. Her zestful approach to learning about print will result in some crayon marks on the table. If this upsets you, just cover the table with newspapers before she begins.

**Means to an end**

A writer needs lots of supplies — and the more varied, the better *(box, right)*. A child's imagination takes her in one direction when she is handed a spiral notebook and pencil, and in a totally different direction when she is given crayons and construction paper. Researchers investigating preschool scribbling were puzzled to find that the children in one study appeared to have begun scribble writing at younger ages than those in another, until they realized that the children in the first group had been handed felt-tip pens, while those in the second had been given crayons, which are tools for drawing, not writing.

Base your choice of writing supplies on what seems best suited to your own child's ability. The thick pencils and crayons that are specially made for preschoolers hold up better under the heavy pressure applied by the fist grip many youngsters use, but they are not easier to grasp, particularly after children switch to a more conventional grip. For many preschoolers, regular pencils and crayons will be a better choice. As an economy measure and convenience, you might want to recycle such items as used envelopes, junk-mail letters, brown paper bags, and shirt cardboards for use as writing paper.

You may also want to buy a small desk or low table for your child to work on; this will please her greatly, as will a chalkboard or an easel. A large piece of paper taped to a wall will give her an excellent stand-up workspace — a good idea if she finds it tiresome to sit for more than a few minutes at a time.

A comfortable place for reading aloud is very important, so

that your youngster will come to associate reading with pleasure and relaxation. This could be an overstuffed chair, a bed, or simply pillows laid on the floor.

If you have a typewriter sturdy enough to withstand some pounding, she will undoubtedly relish using it. Watching the letters appear as if by magic on the paper will reinforce her sense that print moves from left to right. And if you look over what she has typed, chances are you will be able to point out words she has inadvertently typed out.

**Using a computer**

To a child — and perhaps some others — a computer seems like an ideal cross between two interesting things, a typewriter and a television. It has buttons and keys to push; it beeps and grunts, and little lights flash on and off; the screen can project bright colors and sometimes the thing will play musical sounds or even tunes a child can recognize. Because of its inherent attraction, a computer has enormous potential as a tool for teaching about reading and writing. Children who otherwise might be reluctant to sit down and write often can be lured into working with a computer. A simple word-processing program will allow your youngster to have a lot of fun while practicing her letter and symbol recognition and spelling. And while your three-year-old, banging away on that old typewriter, might accidentally make a word or two, your five-year-old at the computer will now know enough to start purposefully crafting words and perhaps even short sentences.

At the same time, however, a computer has its limitations,

## The Right Preschool

While the primary purpose of a preschool should not be to teach reading and writing, a well-designed program can enhance a child's already considerable language skills by providing ample opportunity for her to use reading and writing in her daily activities.

The soundest preschool programs are based on the knowledge that children learn best from firsthand experience. Youngsters so happily engaged in organized or free-play activities that they take little notice of visitors are a good indicator of the effectiveness of the program. When visiting preschools, observe the importance of written language in the room; in addition to play dough, sand, and other materials to touch, pour, sift, mold, pound, and manipulate, there should be lots of printed material around to provide opportunities for the same kind of experimentation with language.

Some points for you to consider when selecting a preschool for your child are:

● *Books:* Is storytime a part of the center's daily schedule? Is there a reading area in which a variety of books is readily available to children to look through at other times during the day? Does the selection of books change regularly? Are the books readily accessible on child-high bookshelves, and are they kept in good repair? Is there a display of books related to the theme of the week's activities? Such displays prompt youngsters to turn to books to learn more about subjects that interest them. Are children encouraged to make their own books — both as a group and individually? Such books might range from a story written by the class to a book by a youngster on everything he knows about dinosaurs.

● *Writing and drawing:* Is there an area set aside for children to draw and write independently during their free-play time? Such a center should feature easels and art supplies for drawing and painting; there should be a table and chairs, and a variety of writing supplies for writing notes to Grandma, making birthday cards for friends, or just experimenting with making *Xs* and *Os*. The center might include lists of words such as *Dear* or *Love* for children to refer to in their writing. Is the children's artwork displayed prominently, and does it include labels written or dictated by the young artists themselves?

and it should never be considered a substitute for a supply of interesting books. If you are fortunate enough to own one, go ahead and let your child hunt and peck for letters. But there is no need to worry that she will fall behind other children if she does not have access to one.

A computer's effectiveness depends solely on the quality of the software you decide to use with it. Some children's programs are good, others are little more than video workbooks. Unfortunately, most computer programs are relatively expensive, and it is difficult to judge their value until you have actually spent some time trying them out. Check your library for computer-magazine articles that rate children's software. And before buying a program, take a look at it. No matter how appealing the graphics may be, ask yourself, "Is it versatile?" Some programs are so simple that your child will grow bored with them quickly.

Another drawback to computers is that, like television, they take your preschooler away from activities that build firsthand knowledge of the world. Counting balloons on a computer screen is fine, but it is no substitute for what she will learn by blowing up a real balloon by herself, by trying to keep it up in the air, or by watching it cling to a wall when it is full of static electricity.

Finally, remember that computer use is as limited as any other literacy-related activity: It cannot possibly substitute for the loving communication that you and your youngster share with each other. ∴

---

- *Signs:* Is the classroom awash in signs? These should not be limited to signs designating the writing area or reading corner but might label supplies on shelves or offer reminders such as, "Please put books back on the shelf." Signs also may be made by the children themselves, with word cards assembled from a readily available selection, so that a young block architect can leave a "DO NOT TOUCH" sign in front of her unfinished structure and be assured that it will be there when she returns.

- *Charts and schedules:* Does the classroom feature a general daily schedule, perhaps with drawings to help youngsters with the written words, so that children can see when storytime or outside playtime comes each day? Typically, there will also be a monthly calendar on which birthdays and holidays are recorded. The class will look at the schedule and calendar, talking about the weather, the changing seasons, or forthcoming special events. This gives the children the opportunity to use written words to learn about the days of the week and the passage of time. A helper's chart is likely to be the most popular item in the classroom, announcing the names of the youngsters chosen for each day's coveted positions of fish feeder, table setter or milk distributor. The children learn quickly to recognize not only their own names, but those of their classmates.

- *Dramatic play:* Does the play area contain not only imaginative costumes and castaway household items but also magazines, menus, message pads, and typewriters for children to incorporate into their scenarios?

- *Visits and visitors:* Does the school take field trips to the local fire department or pet shop, and do various professionals come to the school to talk about what they do for a living? Such programs are excellent for widening the youngsters' view of the world.

- *Activities:* Are the children given plenty of opportunities to choose individual activities and to play freely with each other? And are they encouraged and helped to use language to express their feelings and frustrations during the inevitable altercations? Understanding the power of language to resolve problems is important but often difficult for youngsters to learn.

# Fun and Games with Letters and Words

The simple games and diversions described on the following pages have been designed to develop and strengthen your child's reading-related skills, such as recognition of letters and awareness of the sounds in printed words. These pre-reading activities will work best if they are treated as fun, not as educational drills. Use them as opportunities for your child to play with reading, to have fun with it while practicing literacy skills. By themselves, the activities cannot teach him to read, and they are not intended to do so. They can, however, provide a pleasant supplement to his other experiences with written language and can encourage him to think of reading as an enjoyable pastime.

These games are presented in order of relative difficulty. The activities on this and the next page involve identifying letters. Those on pages 88-89 call for identifying letters within words, which takes greater skill. Some require the players to recognize initial consonant sounds (consonants, unlike vowels, produce relatively consistent sounds and are easier for preschoolers to grasp). Others ask the children to identify sounds within words, a more challenging task, and to make words, which is harder still.

As you watch your child's reading-related skills grow, you can choose the letter and word games he will most enjoy, and profit from, at each level of his development.

## Sandpaper Letters

This activity helps your child become familiar with letter shapes by identifying them with his hand. The use of sandpaper adds texture that makes them more appealing to your child's inquisitive touch. Create a set of alphabet cards by cutting letters out of fine-grain sandpaper and gluing each to an index card. Invite your child to run his hand over the letters to familiarize himself with them. Then put them into a bag or shoebox or some other container and challenge your youngster to reach in, pick a letter, and identify it by touch alone. If you use a shoebox, you can cut a hole in one end so that he will be able to slip his hand into the box without removing the lid and seeing the letter.

## Find the Letter Blindfolded

This is another activity that encourages your youngster to recognize letter shapes by touch as well as by sight. Begin by showing your child a printed letter. Then put a blindfold on him, spread out three or four plastic letters in front of him on the floor or table, and ask him to find the letter you have just shown him.

## Alphabet Road

Designed for three players, this activity requires a separate game board for each. The boards can be simple squares of posterboard, with a path or road drawn across them (below). The paths should be divided into twenty-six segments each, to correspond with the letters of the alphabet. The players share a letter grab bag containing three or four of each letter. You can write letters on small squares of posterboard or use the wooden tiles from a crossword game. (If you do, be sure that you have one letter for each segment — three complete alphabets.)

The first player takes a letter from the bag and puts it down on the correct path segment. If she picks a *J,* for example, she should place it on the tenth segment of her road. The players take turns drawing and placing letters until they have filled in all twenty-six spaces on their boards. If a player draws a letter that she has already placed, she puts it back into the bag and draws again. The first player to complete the alphabet wins the game. The game not only teaches children to recognize individual letters, it also helps to familiarize them with the concept of the alphabet as a series of letters in a specific order.

## Glue a Letter

This is a letter formation game with two levels of difficulty. Both versions require sheets of brightly colored construction paper, glue, and materials that can be stuck to the paper, such as rice, uncooked beans, corn kernels, or dry pasta of various shapes. Cotton balls and miniature marshmallows are also good, and so is colored salt, which you can make by stirring salt in a bowl with pulverized colored chalk.

For the easier version of the game, print large letters on separate sheets of paper, then have your child dip her finger in a saucer of liquid glue and trace

over your letter with her sticky fingertip. Wipe her fingertip clean with a damp cloth and then have her fix the rice or other dried foods to the glue-covered letter.

For the more advanced version of this game, do not write the letters for your child. Let her dip her finger in the glue and trace her own letters on blank sheets of paper. Then have her sprinkle the rice on the glue. When she has produced all the letters of her name, or an entire alphabet of letters, you can mount her handiwork on the walls of her bedroom or in some other conspicuous place for all to see.

### Fishing for Letters
Make a set of alphabet puzzle cards for your child by writing the letters of the alphabet on a set of twenty-six index cards. On each card print the letter in both uppercase and lowercase, leaving a good space between the two. Then attach a metal paper clip to each card and scatter the letters a few at a time on the floor. Give your child a homemade fishing pole consisting of a stick with a magnet hanging by a piece of string from one end *(above)*. The pole can be a ruler, yardstick, or short piece of wood you pick up outdoors. Your child fishes for the letters one at a time, using the magnet to "catch" the paper clip fastened to each card. As he yanks up

a letter, ask him what he has caught and give him as much help as he needs to identify the letter.

### Alphabet Puzzle Match
Make a set of letter cards similar to those used in Fishing for Letters. Then cut each card in half, making the cut curved or jagged so the two halves will fit together like puzzle pieces. Your child can then match the uppercase and lowercase versions of each letter by fitting the puzzle cards correctly together.

### Draw and Guess
To play this group game, you will need a writing surface that is easy to erase for frequent reuse, such as a magic slate or a chalkboard. Each player takes a turn writing a letter and concealing the writing surface so the others cannot see it. The writer then gives clues that describe the letter, and the players try to guess what she has written. She might describe her letter by saying, "It has one circle and one line," ($Q$); or "It has two straight lines and one slanty line," ($N$ or $Z$); or "If you turn it upside down, it looks like an $M$," ($W$). As soon as someone guesses correctly, the writer shows her letter to the other players, and another child takes a turn writing.

### Pipe Cleaner Letters
Children like bending fuzzy, flexible, colorful pipe cleaners into a variety of shapes. In this game, the pipe cleaners are used to improve letter-forming skills. Give your youngster several pipe cleaners and encourage her to twist them into uppercase and lowercase letters, copying the letter shapes from alphabet cards or from any other printed source you provide for her. When the activity is over, she can straighten out the pipe cleaners and store them away to be used again later.

### Design a Letter Poster
Give your child an old magazine or newspaper. Write down a letter (both its uppercase and lowercase versions) on a sheet of construction paper. Have him cut out that letter, from headlines, adver-

tisements, or anywhere else he might find it. He will soon discover that a letter can vary in its appearance while still meaning the same thing. When your youngster has assembled a good-size collection of letters, he can make a poster by gluing letters to the paper.

### Outline Puzzle
Place three plastic letters on three index cards and trace around the letters with a pencil. Give your child the cards and letters separately and have her match the letters to their pencil outlines.

### Bathtub Letter Game
Bathtime can be a wonderful occasion for learning through play. You can use it as an opportunity to help your child become familiar with letters. As he is sitting in the tub, use the tip of one finger to trace a letter on his bare back *(below)*. Ask him what letter you have "written" there. When he is very young, you can make the game easy by sticking to the simplest letters, such as $O$, $T$ and $L$, or by asking questions that help him narrow down his choices: "Am I writing an $A$ or a $B$ on your back?" As he grows older, you can include more letters in the game and you can gradually stop helping him with clues.

## Picture-Word Cards

To make a set of cards for this game, cut out an assortment of magazine pictures of objects whose names begin with various consonants. Glue the pictures to index cards, and under each picture write the name of the object, omitting the first letter. Give the cards to your child, along with a set of wooden letter tiles from a crossword game or of homemade letter squares cut from stiff paper or cardboard. The object of the game is to identify each picture and select the missing consonant to complete the word by picking the correct letter from the tiles or squares.

## Go Fish

This is a variation on the popular card game. To make a Go Fish deck, simply choose thirteen simple words and write each one on four index cards, for a total of fifty-two cards. Shuffle this deck, deal seven cards to each player, and set the rest of the deck down where everyone can reach it. Before play begins, players discard any pairs in their hands. Then the first player asks some other player, "Please give me all your cards that say *cat,*" or whatever word he is trying to match. If the player who has been asked has a cat card, he hands it over. If not, he says, "Go fish," and the player who asked for a card draws from the top of the deck. Then the second player asks someone for a card, and so on. Whenever a player gets a matching card from another player, or draws it from the deck,

he discards the pair. The first player to get rid of all his cards wins the game. For younger children, this game can be played with letters instead of words.

## Supermarket

For this game, you will need three grocery bags, each with a different letter written on the outside, and an assortment of groceries and other purchases beginning with those three letters. Pretend to go shopping with your child, and have him pick up and put into the bag those items that begin with the letters on the bag.

## Word Search Poster

Here, your child will be making a poster with cutout words. Begin by going through some old magazines and cutting out a large assortment of words. Be sure to choose words that start with a variety of consonants. Then print a letter (capital and lowercase) on a chalkboard, and tell your child to look through your pile of words and select the ones that begin with that letter. Have her glue those she has chosen onto a piece of construction paper. If she is willing, in the days ahead, have her make other posters using different consonants. Later, when your child has enough experience with written language to identify individual words (be-

cause they are separated by spaces), she can go through the magazines on her own, cutting out the words she will need for new posters.

## I'm Thinking of Something That Begins With . . .

This initial consonant game needs no equipment, which makes it a favorite on long car trips. Each player in turn thinks of an object, usually something in sight, and announces its initial letter or sound. For example, a player would say, "I'm thinking of something that begins with *T.*" The other players try to guess the object. If necessary, the player who is thinking of the object can give additional clues.

## Collecting First Letters

The equipment required is a bag containing twenty letter cards bearing consonants only. Each player draws a card from the bag in turn and tries to find an object in the room beginning with that letter. If he can name such an object, he keeps the letter; otherwise, he has to return it to the bag. When the bag is empty, the player who has collected the most letters wins.

## I Packed My Grandmother's Trunk

Besides helping to teach initial letters (both vowels and consonants), this game gives your child an amusing way to learn the alphabet. The first player says, "I packed my grandmother's trunk with an *A,*" and then names something that begins with *A* —

an apple, for instance. Each player after that repeats what has already been named and adds an object beginning with the next letter of the alphabet. The second player might say, "I packed my grandmother's trunk with an apple and a *B,* a balloon." With older children, the game can proceed through all twenty-six letters. With younger children, parents might want to limit it to the first five to ten letters.

Like the "I'm Thinking of Something That Begins with . . ." game, this one can be played as a diversion on a trip. Children will keep themselves busy for long periods, filling grandma's trunk and giggling over the silly objects they think of to pack in it.

### Pictures and Letters

The cards you will need for this game are just like the ones you made for "Picture-Word Cards" — magazine pictures glued onto index cards. Do not write the names of the objects under the pictures, however. Be sure to make enough cards so that each player will have six to eight. To begin, deal out the cards, laying them face up in front of each child. Players then take turns drawing consonants from a bag of wooden letter tiles or homemade cardboard squares. Each player in turn draws a consonant, and looks to see whether she has a picture of an object beginning with that letter. If so, she lays the tile or square down on the matching card. If not, she returns the tile to the bag. The first player to draw initial consonants for all of her pictures wins. Since many of the pictures on the game cards may begin with the same letter, the grab bag will have to contain enough duplicate tiles to give each player a fair chance to draw all the necessary consonants.

### Rhyming Games

These games use children's natural interest in rhyming words to build vocabulary and develop awareness of the letter sounds that make words rhyme. To play the simplest rhyming game, just say a word and ask your child to respond with a word that rhymes. You can trade rhyming words back and forth — *book, look, hook, took, crook, shook* — until you run out and move on to the next rhyme.

Children also like to play with the sounds of names and will enjoy a name-guessing game with rhyming clues. For example, one player might say, "I'm thinking of a name and it rhymes with tank." The other players then need to guess that the name was Frank. Or children can make up rhymes for names: "Pat, Pat wore a hat," or "Fred, Fred went to bed."

To play a rhyming game with beginning readers, you can write a list of simple words on a piece of paper and use them in a guessing game. One player picks a word from the list and gives a rhyming clue: "I'm thinking of a word that rhymes with tall." The other players take turns guessing: "Is it ball?" "Is it wall?" The player who guesses the word then gives the next clue.

### Names That Rhyme

For this game make pairs of picture cards, using pictures of objects with rhyming names such as cat and hat, shell and bell, dog and frog — and writing the name of each object under the picture. Mix the cards up, then give them to your child and tell her to match the rhyming pairs.

### Letter Sound Placemats

Use this activity to help your preschooler develop an understanding of the relationship between letters and their sounds. Give him a sheet of construction paper with a capital and lowercase letter printed in the middle. Then discuss the sound or sounds the letter can make. Next ask him to cut out pictures of objects that begin with that letter from old magazines. He can glue them to the paper until the space around the letter is filled up. You might invite him to do the same on the reverse side of the paper, using a different letter.

To turn the decorated sheet of construction paper into a durable placemat, sandwich it between two sheets of transparent self-adhesive plastic. Use the placemat at mealtimes, so that your youngster can admire his handiwork and recall the letter-sound lesson at every meal. Vary the challenge by flipping the placemat over from time to time.

### How Does It End?

For this game make picture cards, but do not write the name of each object under its picture. Instead, write three letters, spaced well apart, one of which should be the final letter of the object's name. Ask your youngster to identify the correct final sound for each picture. Be sure to choose objects such as hat, bed, and dog, whose ending sounds are formed by one consonant rather than objects like fish and bath where two consonants together are necessary to pronounce one sound. ❖

# 4 Storytime

It is never too early — and never too late, really — for storytime. One of the enduring joys of childhood is listening to stories — being read to, and looking at the wonderful pictures in the books, or just settling back entranced while a storyteller weaves a magical spell of words.

The storytime magicians for youngsters can be anyone close — parents, of course, and grandparents, other relatives, teachers, siblings, and older friends. The twenty-month-old girl at right is being read to by a boy of nine, a good friend who, despite the age difference, thinks she is a lot of fun to be with. He has become a proficient reader and is sharing his skills with her as she listens and looks at a book about animals.

The toddler is learning a great deal from storytime: what books look and feel like, how ideas are expressed and communicated in ways other than speech, how the sounds of reading differ from the sounds of conversation, how stories — good ones — follow a logical sequence, and how they mirror her own life and help her deal with things. Her vocabulary is expanding, her fund of information growing, her imagination sprouting wings, and her powers of thought gaining strength. All her faculties are in operation.

As the girl grows older, storytime will introduce her to a vast world of books, and they will play an ever increasing role in her life. She will go to bookstores and libraries with her parents, develop favorite themes and subjects, and start a collection of books of her own. Sitting in someone's lap or side by side at storytime, she will discover how writing flows across the pages, where stories begin and end, how letters make words, and how words make sentences. Intrigued and happy, she will be anxious to know more about those marvelous marks. She is learning to read.

# Why Reading Aloud Matters

Most parents enjoy reading aloud to their children as much as the children love being read to — for the simple reason that it involves sharing warm feelings and makes up one of the most peaceful and magical moments of the day. Long afterward, children who were read to on a regular basis preserve vivid associations and happy memories of storytime. Adults often find this a perfect opportunity to introduce their youngster to books and tales that they listened to when they were young.

**Stimulating young imaginations**

One of the greatest pleasures this labor of love can give you is the growing excitement you will see as your reading aloud unlocks your child's imagination. Hearing about a world of talking animals or of imaginary kingdoms inhabited by noble princesses and wicked witches fulfills her need for fantasy, which is almost as basic to her development as her need for love or nourishment. Once her imagination takes flight, she will want you to read to her more and more.

**A boost to learning**

Reading aloud does another wonderful thing: It stimulates an early interest in learning and literature. Basically, it introduces children to many key language concepts crucial to their intellectual development. It also increases their vocabulary and encourages them to experiment with new words and patterns of speech. It also teaches children the mechanics of reading: how to hold a book; how to turn pages; how to proceed from left to right and top to bottom, a page at a time. And when later they learn to read in school, words that they recognize aurally will be easier for them to identify in print than those they have never heard before.

Listening to stories, your child will discern that written language is more formal, more diverse, more melodious than speech. The sounds and cadences, the rhymes, word repetitions, word plays, and whimsical and memorable names — Rotten Ralph, Winnie the Pooh, Amelia Bedelia — used by the authors will all sharpen your youngster's sensitivity to the music and fun of language.

Children whose parents read to them daily learn to pay attention, to remember details, and to formulate questions. Their powers of logic are enhanced. By hearing their favorite books over and over again, toddlers realize that stories must follow a regular sequence, as any parent who has ever tried to skip a portion of one knows. When Mother Duck loses three of her ducklings in their first attempt to swim over a waterfall, do not expect to close the book after only two ducklings have been

*An infant seeks to give his favorite book to his mother while she reads to his older brother. Babies like being read to even though they cannot speak. Early exposure to books in ways like this can lead to a lifelong appreciation of reading.*

found. Your child will insist on hearing one more time what happened to the third duckling — and rightly so. The story world is a vivid world, and the tale holds threat without that missing detail.

Besides strengthening verbal and comprehension skills, reading aloud reaches well beyond the confines of childhood's natural boundaries. Books can take children anywhere — to a farm, to the jungle, to the top of the Eiffel Tower, to a glacier, to a prehistoric swamp inhabited by dinosaurs. Books also enable a child to explore areas of personal interest in depth. They tell how airplanes fly, what a bulldozer does, and how babies are made. From the comfort of your armchair, you and your child can embark on a voyage of discovery together.

**Providing insights**     You can use books to increase your youngster's understanding of herself and society. Her involvement with the characters in the stories will teach her about motivation, good behavior, the difference between right and wrong, and the natural consequences of certain deeds. Books also can shed light on childhood dilemmas — jealousy over the birth of a sibling, grief over the death of a pet, anxiety about the sudden illness of a relative — and present the youngster with acceptable ways to handle their feelings.

Reading aloud engenders in many children their first feelings of compassion or empathy for others, as they grow sad or concerned about characters in their books — a child without friends, a bird that cannot fly. Parents who take the opportunity to discuss such touching stories with their children can use them to reinforce values without preaching.

**Setting the stage**     When choosing books to read aloud, strive for variety. Fantasies, folk tales, poetry, realistic accounts, and funny stories will familiarize your youngster with a range of writing styles, approaches, and information. But in your effort to provide him with a diverse listening experience, be careful to pick books that fit his interest and attention span. Many publishers indicate the age levels for which their books are intended right on the covers, with notice of any awards the works may have received. No matter how well recommended a book may seem, it is a good idea to thumb through it first; if you like the book, chances are your youngster will like it, too.

Once you bring a new book home, give your youngster a little preview of it to pique his interest. If possible, relate the story or content to an experience he has had: "Remember the squirrel we saw in the park yesterday? Well, this story is about a squirrel and her family who live in a nest of leaves on top of the highest tree." If you have selected a book by an author or illustrator whom you and your child have enjoyed before, point out the name to him; it will heighten his anticipation.

**Tips for reading**    Be sure to let your child settle down before starting the book and then read slowly, clearly, and with enthusiasm. Changing your voice to suit the action or the characters will show her that you, too, are enjoying the story. Deliberately pause at the end of sentences or paragraphs to give your listener a chance to think about what she has just heard and to ask any questions. Racing through a book not only betrays a lack of interest but deprives your youngster of an opportunity to satisfy her curiosity about the story. And be alert to your child's reactions and initiatives. No useful purpose is served by your insisting on finishing a book when your little one's attention has plainly waned or when a certain passage or character frightens or upsets her. Dramatically closing a book shows that the unwanted or scary character is "trapped" inside. This lets your child know that she is in control of at least that part of her world.

Children are never too young to enjoy being read to. Just the sound of a nursery rhyme can be pleasing to your newborn's ears. When your baby is a little older, you can sit him in your lap and share a simple book with him. You may feel at first as though you are having a one-sided conversation, but do not be put off — your baby is already developing important storytime associations revolving around your soothing voice and loving embrace. During these early months, what matters is not so much what you read, as how you condition your child to the pleasures of the reading experience.

**What you can expect of infants**

By four months, when many babies have started to respond to pictures, your little one will be fascinated by books with colorful illustrations. But she will be equally fascinated by them as objects and will take great pleasure in chewing and sucking on them. If your baby is teething, offer her something to chew on while you read. If she grabs or tears the pages, put a stuffed animal in her hands. Eventually she will understand that books are not toys and should be treated with respect.

By seven months, your baby will pay attention as you point to pictures and comment on them. If you single out various details in her books, you not only help focus her interest but also extend her attention span. When she points to something on the page, linger there and talk about it. She will be particularly delighted when she spots a familiar object, a doll, or a Teddy bear like her own. Stop frequently to ask her questions and to relate the book to her own life whenever possible. You might remind her that "this ball looks just like the ball Aunt Sharon gave you." Young children love repetition; be willing to repeat the names of the objects in the pictures again and again.

When she reaches twelve months of age, your little one will be filled with energy. Do not be surprised if she sits in your lap for only a minute while you are reading, then wants to be put down so she can crawl or toddle about the room. This does not necessarily reflect a lack of interest: It may merely be her way of expressing her excitement over what she is hearing. But if she fusses or turns away as you read, put the volume on the shelf and come back to it another time.

Toddlers like being directly involved in the reading experience. Let yours turn the pages, if that is what he wants. Or let him choose his own story. He may pick the same one several days running and expect you to reread it with all the enthusiasm you had the first time. You should recognize that familiarity with the story is not a drawback — it only increases his enjoyment. He will be proud of his ability to identify items in the pictures. You might make a game out of rereading by omitting words and letting him supply them.

*Cuddled by his mother, this active toddler soon wanders from her side but returns for her embrace, proof that he has been listening all the while. However short their attention spans, toddlers can still enjoy and benefit from storytime. Brief, frequent sessions suit them best.*

# Parent to Parent

## The Joys of the Reading Experience

❝ At nine months of age all Max wants to do with books is to gum them to death. If I give him something to chew on when I'm reading to him, he'll last about five minutes. But just let him see a picture of something he recognizes, like a red ball — he hits the page and wants to get off my lap to look for his own ball. So far we've had the most success with old magazines. He loves their bright colors and he happily turns the pages — and I don't have to worry about his messing them up. ❞

❝ When Benjamin was about two, he began to bite his little friends. I discovered some children's books on biting and I read them to him. We had lots of conversations in a neutral atmosphere when neither of us was emotional. Those biting books helped solve our problem, and I've passed them on to others. ❞

❝ When I was a child no one ever made reading much fun. It wasn't until I was a teenager that I got hooked on books. So I was anxious for David to learn from the start what a treat reading is. We go to the library once a week, and for him it's just as exciting now as going to a candy store. He can't wait until we get home so we can sit down and read together. ❞

❝ I've had to personalize our reading ritual since my two boys are so close in age that they share everything — toys, clothes, a room. Before bedtime each chooses three books and I lie on Thomas's bed with him first and read his choices. Then I move to the other bed and devote myself to Dan. They can listen to each others' books if they wish to, but I concentrate on the son whose turn it is. If their choices are the same, I simply read the story twice — on two different beds. ❞

❝ Neither Daniel nor Stevie is a particularly good eater and so we read to them at mealtime. For them, hearing another book is a better incentive to finish their meal than dessert is. In fact, in our house, books are desserts. ❞

❝ Storytime at our house can be pretty noisy. Usually I read to Nicole, our five-year-old, and my husband, Mike, does the sound effects. It's almost like the old days, when families sat around listening to the radio. Mike has mastered the simple things such as knocking and the wind blowing. It's when he has to think up the sound a camel makes or something like that that he has to be creative. And by the time the story has ended, we all end up laughing on Nicole's bed. I love seeing her go to sleep so happy. ❞

**Satisfying inquisitive preschoolers**

At the preschool stage, your child's quickly developing language skills, coupled with his natural curiosity, will lead him to ask innumerable questions. In fact, you may be unnerved by having so many popped at you as you try to read. At such moments, be patient; you will get to the end of the story sooner or later. In the meantime, it is more important to answer your child's questions. You will not only be pleasing your child, but you will also be enhancing his intellect; he will absorb the new information, and in a process known as scaffolding, he will match and integrate it with what he already knows, creating new mental structures from ones that exist.

As a way of further involving him, encourage your youngster to actively comment on the story and the characters by posing questions that challenge his imagination, rather than those that require only one-word answers. You might ask, "What do you think monkeys do at their birthday parties?" Or "Why does the duckling feel sad?" In the middle of an adventure, ask your child to predict what will happen next. Reinforce his response to an illustration with a correctly worded but helpful reply, such as, "Yes, a big black dog with white spots is in the sandbox." If he identifies the animal as a cat, you can elaborate, "Yes, cats have spots too, but dogs are bigger and they bark." After you have finished reading the book to your youngster, you might invite him to hold the book himself and retell the story.

As your preschooler begins to commit to memory his favorite stories, he will love "reading" them aloud to you. This gives him a strong sense of accomplishment, and you should do everything you can to encourage it. Plainly, he now connects the stories with written text rather than with the pictures, a great stride forward in his development.

**Alternatives to reading aloud**

You may not always be able to read to your child in person, yet you may still want the reading routine to go on during your absence. Some parents tape books for their children to listen to while they are away on trips. If you make such a recording, be sure to include a brief message letting your youngster know that you are reading the story just for him and be sure to put in the special effects that amuse him. Homemade tapes can also be used to remind children of distant, loving relatives. A tape of Grandma reading from one of her own favorite books can bring enormous pleasure to a child and strengthen family ties.

There are, of course, many excellent children's recordings. Some come with picture books so that a child can "read" along with them. Others combine music and text. *The Carnival of the Animals* by Camille Saint-Saëns, with poems and narration by the famous British playwright Noel Coward, is a prime example. Fine as these options may be, regard them only as supplements to your read-aloud sessions.

**When reading begins**

Storytime should not end once your child learns to read in school. Indeed, being read to promotes, rather than retards, his desire to read on his own. Soon, of course, he will be too big to sit on your lap. But even then he will continue to enjoy your reading time together as one of life's happiest moments. ❖

*Listening to a story on tape, a relaxed girl follows the action in the accompanying book. Homemade tapes of favorite stories, with a personal message added, can supplement live read-aloud sessions or substitute for television.*

97

# The Wide World of Children's Books

The books you choose for your youngster will have an enormous effect on the development of her reading and writing skills — to say nothing of her enjoyment and view of life. Sharing books will together establish a pattern of intellectual fulfillment and companionship that will remain to the end of her days. And so it is important for you to have a solid working knowledge of children's books and to be equipped to evaluate the field in light of your little one's needs and desires.

There are thousands of children's books on the market; it is a rich literature, wide-ranging and characterized by marvelous art. You will have no trouble at all finding a broad variety that will allow your budding reader to reap the full benefits of books. You will want some that are serious and some that are humorous, some that offer real-life stories and some that delve into fantasy. You will probably want to mix the great classics with modern books and build a library of various types of books — storybooks, songbooks, Mother Goose rhymes, informational books, and of course, books of poetry. Although adults may overlook children's poetry, youngsters themselves enjoy it tremendously.

**What to look for**

In choosing a book for your child, you should naturally like it yourself. After all, you will be reading and sharing it with him. And you will want to be sure to match it to his interests and level of development. The American Library Association awards annual medals to the authors and illustrators of children's books; the Newbery Medal honors a meritorious author, while the Caldecott Medal goes to a distinguished illustrator. Any book so highly recommended is worth your consideration.

All children seem to thrive on stories about other children or about animals that behave as children, and they like books in which characters face situations children face, or books that have familiar settings, such as a home. In addition to content, you will want to look at language. Nonsense rhymes will tickle your toddler, but not long, abstract descriptions. Try reading a section of the book aloud to see if the words sound natural to the ear; if they do to yours, they will to his. Trace the plot of the story; it should flow clearly from one event to the next and end on a satisfying note. In general, stories for young children should deal with familiar concepts, but that does not mean that they have to be simple-minded. Your toddler does not have to be a psychologist to get a kick out of Maurice Sendak's *Where the Wild Things Are,* in which Max puts on a wolf suit and gets sent to his room for acting wild, then imagines himself ruling over an island full of wild creatures.

Look at how the book uses pictures and how it is laid out. See if the illustrations appear on the page with the appropriate text. And judge whether the pictures match the text. Children can be as literal as anybody else; if the book says the truck is red, they expect the truck in the picture to be red.

You surely will want to share the books you remember fondly from your own childhood. But do not always choose your child's books for him; he will like picking out some on his own and you will learn more about what he finds interesting.

You will find that many bookstores have large children's departments, with much to choose from. Libraries are also good places for book-hunting expeditions: They are likely to have even more children's books than a store. Try making a trip to the local library once a week, and when you find books your child asks for again and again, consider buying them for his private collection.

Book clubs also can be a good source of children's books. Before ordering, make sure that you can return books you or your child finds inadequate. If you are familiar with a book, you can let him open the carton when it arrives; but if you ordered a book based on the blurb in the club brochure, you may want to take a look before your child does. That way, he will not be so disappointed if you find it unsatisfactory or think that he is not quite ready for it.

Many publishers print a recommended age range on a book's cover or dust jacket. This can be helpful, yet there may be times when you will want a somewhat advanced book to challenge your youngster and give him something to grow into.

*Although years must pass before she becomes a reader, books are already a part of this baby's day. An accordion-folded board book stands alone in the crib and fascinates the infant with its high-contrast colors and varied shapes.*

# Books for Infants (Birth to Twelve Months)

Ahlberg, Janet, and Allan Ahlberg, *Peek-a-Boo!* Have your young child peek through the book's cutout circles in order to see what the baby sees.

Campbell, Rod, *Dear Zoo.* Letters to the zoo asking for a pet bring the wrong animals until just the right one comes along. See also *Oh Dear!,* in which a child helps Grandma find eggs at a farm; your little one assists by lifting the pop-up flaps.

DePaola, Tomie, *Tomie DePaola's Mother Goose.* Favorite rhymes, wonderfully illustrated.

Freeman, Don, *Corduroy Goes to the Doctor.* Adapted and illustrated by Lisa McCue. A board book in which a lovable bear goes to the doctor for a checkup.

Hill, Eric, *Spot's First Words; Spot Looks at Colors; Spot Looks at Shapes; Spot at the Farm; Spot at the Fair; Spot at Play.* In this series of board books, your young one can point to and identify the places and things in Spot's world.

Hoban, Tana, *Red, Blue, Yellow Shoe.* A board book of marvelous photographs of objects labeled by color. You and your child also can point to and label things in *Is It Larger? Is It Smaller?* and *Is It Red? Is It Yellow? Is It Blue?* See also *Panda, Panda* for a fun-filled look at a young panda rolling, hiding, and playing.

Oxenbury, Helen, *Dressing; Family; Friends; Playing.* Board books depicting a child dressing herself, being with her family, being with friends, and having fun playing. Also look for *Shopping Trip; Mother's Helper; Beach Day; Good Night;* and *Good Morning.* In *Tickle, Tickle; Clap Hands; Say Goodnight;* and *All Fall Down,* a multicultural group of children have loads of fun.

Wells, Rosemary, *Max's First Word; Max's Ride; Max's Toys: A Counting Book;* and *Max's New Suit.* Board books about an adorable imp who has a mind of his own. Also look for *Max's Bath; Max's Birthday; Max's Breakfast;* and *Max's Bedtime.*

Wildsmith, Brian, *Brian Wildsmith's Mother Goose.* Vivid colors and designs illustrate the great old rhymes.

Ziefert, Harriet, *Bear Gets Dressed; Bear All Year; Bear Goes Shopping; Bear's Busy Morning.* Illustrated by Arnold Lobel. Your child plays a guessing game with Bear as she folds out pictures to reveal the answers.

**Your child's first books**

You can start reading to your baby even before you are home from the hospital. At two months, she will be lifting her head and looking around; now is the time to put something interesting in her crib — a book with large pictures or designs. Dick Bruna's *My Toys* is a zig-zag book and is easy to prop up; it has simple pictures and bright colors.

When your infant is about three months old, you can hold her on your lap to read to her. Both songs and Mother Goose rhymes will please her, and you may now want to start a collection of Mother Goose and songbooks. They will be among her favorite books for several years, so they should be sturdy.

Tomie De Paola's *Mother Goose* has big, bright pictures, and Brian Wildsmith's *Mother Goose* has vivid purples, fuchsias, and hexagonal shapes. *Mother Goose: The Old Nursery Rhymes,* illustrated by the famed Arthur Rackham, offers three types of illustrations: pen-and-ink, silhouettes, and full-page color pictures. *The Real Mother Goose,* illustrated by Blanche Fisher Wright, has a color picture on each page and characters wearing period costumes. In addition, you might want to look at some modern books, such as *The Baby's Lap Book* by Kay Charao and *Catch Me, Kiss Me and Say It Again* by Clyde and Wendy Watson.

At about six months, your baby will be sitting up and grabbing at everything. Give her some books to explore — and bang and chew. As the soft pages of cloth books are hard to turn, you may want to consider hard cardboard books with wipe-clean surfaces and rounded corners. Hard-cover books also come in small sizes resembling blocks. Lydia Freeman's *Corduroy's Toys* is a sturdy, pudgy little book with bright colors, just right for baby hands.

As your child approaches nine months, she will be ready for books inviting her to point out objects in pictures, and soon she will say their names. *Colors to Know* and *Shapes to Show* by Karen Gundersheimer are lively learning books. And with one word per page Tana Hoban's board book *Panda Panda* introduces such words as *eating, playing,* and *hiding* through pictures of a young panda.

**The toddler's library**

Between your youngster's first and second birthdays, his ability with language will burst forth. He will love to jabber and to rattle off the names of things, and pretty soon his favorite word will be *why.*

He will enjoy stories more now, ones that reflect his own eventful life — tales about messy eaters, children who bump their heads, or who get lost and then are found again. *Ask Mr. Bear* by Marjorie Flack, tells of a child asking all the animals what he should get his mother for her birthday. Mr. Bear finally comes up with the answer — a big bear hug. In Margaret Wise Brown's classic *Goodnight Moon,* a bunny child says good night to all his favorite things. As the bunny gets sleepier, the illustrations grow darker.

As your little one pores over the pictures in his books, he will be getting his first real look at the world of art. Illustrations can now become more detailed and convey more information. He will most readily recognize pictures from his everyday life, but some experts think it is good also to expose toddlers to abstract forms and muted colors as a way of encouraging a developing appreciation of diversity.

If you keep your toddler's books on low tables or shelves where he is able to reach them, they will become a regular part of his day. He will enjoy carrying them around, looking at them on the floor, showing them to his friends or members of his family, and bringing them to you to read.

*Sharing a book can be extra special when the pages stretch across two laps. The wide format of this toddler's storybook allows mother and daughter to sit side-by-side and take in the expansive illustrations together. Books of different sizes and shapes should be a part of your little one's library.*

**Early learning books**   Your youngster's library should now include books that take her on voyages of discovery — books that describe activities and invite her to participate. Dorothy Kunhardt's *Pat the Bunny* has long been a favorite among toddlers and parents; it will take your child on an expedition of sensory adventures — stroking a furry bunny, smelling flowers, trying on a ring, feeling a father's scratchy beard. Other early learning books focus on sound, encouraging your child to mimic the noises of the animals and objects she sees in the pictures. *Pigs Say Oink: A First Book of Sounds* by Martha Alexander features day and night, and city and country sounds. By lifting the flaps in Eric Hill's *Spot's First Walk,* you and your youngster can search for the adventurous puppy.

An ABC book at this stage will help make the letters of the alphabet familiar and show how written symbols represent sound. Your youngster need not be ready to learn the alphabet to use an alphabet book: A two-year-old can point out and name the objects in the pictures, and later she will say the letters along with the objects' names. A good ABC book employs pictures of things your child recognizes easily. Thomas Matthiesen's *ABC: An Alphabet Book* and C. B. Fall's *The ABC Book* both contain one clear, color photograph representing each letter. Beatrix Potter's *Peter Rabbit's ABC* is a charming compilation of elements from her paintings, some previously unpublished. And in Suse MacDonald's *Alphabatics,* each letter contorts and

## An Expert's View

### The Essential Fairy Tale

Recently, many parents and educators have questioned the wisdom of reading fairy-tale classics to young children, arguing that the traditional stories communicate outmoded ideas. Complaining of excessive violence, value systems that equate evil with ugliness and goodness with beauty, and the reliance on magical solutions of problems, some parents read bowdlerized editions or censor the tales. But these well-meaning revisionists are missing the point: Today, the classics make the same positive contribution toward helping children cope with the problems of growing up that they have for centuries.

For a story to enrich a child's life, it must stimulate his imagination, help develop his intellect and clarify his emotions, and be attuned to his anxieties while suggesting solutions to his problems. In short, the story must relate directly to him. When it does, there is little that can be more satisfying.

Why? Because fairy tales reflect a child's view of the world. In every story, the hero or heroine is thrust into dangers. This is exactly how youngsters see life, even when in reality their own lives proceed favorably. To the four-to-six-year old, life seems to be a sequence of periods of smooth living unexpectedly threatened by immense dangers, as when a loving parent suddenly turns gruff and makes a seemingly unreasonable demand. By identifying with the hero or heroine in the tales, the child learns that he must face life's trials on his own. Most importantly, the inevitable happy ending teaches him that if he tries hard enough and is courageous and virtuous, he will be rewarded for his efforts. He realizes that despite all tribulations (such as desertion by the parents in *Hansel and Gretel* or the devouring anger of the giant in *Jack and the Beanstalk*) not only will he succeed, but the evil forces will be done away with forever.

Any youngster who has heard the original fairy tales will rightly reject the prettified versions. For example, it is bound to strike him as inappropriate that Cinderella should forgive her sisters, as she does in some modern revisions. He feels unequivocally that the wicked should be punished.

It is my hope that with a proper understanding of the unique merits of the classic fairy tales, parents and teachers will once again assign them a central role in the life of the child.

*Bruno Bettelheim*
*Professor Emeritus of Psychology and Psychiatry*
*University of Chicago*

## Books for Toddlers (Ages One to Three Years)

Ahlberg, Janet, and Allan Ahlberg, *Each Peach Pear Plum.* Play "I Spy" with nursery-rhyme characters.

Barton, Byron, *Boats; Trains; Airplanes; Trucks.* Four simple informational books about ways to travel and transport things. Good for pointing at the pictures and labeling.

Brown, Margaret Wise, *Goodnight Moon.* Illustrated by Clement Hurd. A wonderful sleepytime story in which a young bunny says good night to all the things in his room.

Carle, Eric, *The Very Hungry Caterpillar.* All about the people foods a hungry caterpillar eats. Have your youngster poke her finger through the holes he leaves; watch the caterpillar turn into a huge butterfly.

Crews, Donald, *Freight Train.* Strong graphic designs identify the parts of a train. Also look for *Truck,* in the same vein, and *Ten Black Dots,* a counting book.

Hill, Eric, *Where's Spot?* Lift the flaps to find the puppy, Spot, and his playthings. Some adventures include *Spot's First Walk; Spot at the Circus; Spot Goes to School;* and *Spot Goes to the Beach.*

Jonas, Ann, *Now We Can Go.* How a youngster collects all her favorite toys to take along on a short outing away from home. Also look for *Where Can It Be?,* a tale of a child's search for that special blanket.

Kunhardt, Dorothy, *Pat the Bunny.* A classic participation book that invites your youngster to experience various textures.

Maris, Ron, *Is Anyone Home?* Lift the flaps to see what a child discovers on a visit to Grandma and Grandpa. See also *Are You There, Bear?* and *My Book.*

Martin, Bill Jr., *Brown Bear, Brown Bear, What Do You See?* Illustrated by Eric Carle. A rhythmic refrain that children can "read" alone after hearing a few times.

Ormerod, Jan, *Sunshine* and *Moonlight.* Wordless stories of a girl and her family.

Rockwell, Anne, and Harlow Rockwell, *My Dentist; My Doctor; The Toolbox; Supermarket.* Superbly designed picture books full of things for children to identify.

Tafuri, Nancy, *Have You Seen My Duckling?* Children help Mother Duck spot her impish runabout duckling.

---

transforms itself into an object beginning with that letter.

You might get your child a counting book to foster an awareness of symbols for numbers and of numbers in series. Counting books range from those that present the numbers one to ten with simple pictures to those that tell a story or feature an artist's imaginative depictions. Molly Bang's *Ten, Nine, Eight* is a countdown book especially suited to the bedtime story session.

Other concept books can teach your toddler basic shapes, colors, and sizes, thus building her language skills and knowledge of the world around her. Tana Hoban's *Look Again* will show your child the world through a photographer's eye. Plain white pages with small holes reveal only part of the larger photograph on the next page. In this way, each preceding page invites your child to guess what she will see next.

Then there are numerous books written to help children learn about daily living and answer the ever-present "why?" You can find books to help your child prepare for her first trip to the dentist — Anne and Harlow Rockwell's *My Dentist* is an excellent example — or for visiting that special doctor who needs to check her tonsils. Other books explain how supermarkets operate, how bicycles work, how factories run, how birds fly, how thunderstorms form, and how the seasons come and go.

**About picture books**    You may hear a bookstore clerk refer to almost any children's book as a picture book, but the true picture book is one in which the illustrations help tell the story. The pictures pick up where the text leaves off, and each is richer for the other's presence.

Such books will galvanize your child's imagination and greatly enhance his skill at interpreting and telling stories. As you explore these books together, you can talk about all the different things you see.

Some good examples of the genre are Gail Gibbons's *Check It Out,* about libraries, and *Fill It Up,* about gas stations. In *The Milk Makers,* Gibbons uses pictures and simple words to show how milk comes from cows and travels to the dairy.

In picture books with text, be sure the pictures and words go together harmoniously. Pat Hutchins's *Rosie's Walk* uses twelve double-page spreads and thirty-two words to tell the story of a hen's journey through the barnyard while a fox sneaks stealthily after her. Though the text never mentions the fox, the pictures show how he repeatedly just misses catching Rosie and how he finally gets his comeuppance.

**Changing needs**

The books your toddler loves will continue to hold her interest all through her preschool years. But as she grows older, she will be ready to handle increasingly complicated and sophisticated stories. In fact, a rousing good story will become very important to her, and she will want it to have a well-constructed plot, sympathetic characters, nicely-paced narrative, and clear climax. She is beginning to sort out the world around her and to exercise her critical senses. "Jack and the Beanstalk," "The Three Little Pigs," and "The Three Billy Goats Gruff" are just right at this time. A little later, she might enjoy Graham Oakley's *The Church Mice and the Moon,* a zany adventure in which a group of mice and a cat outsmart some over ambitious scientists. And some excellent books deal with serious subjects. Judith Viorst's *The Tenth Good Thing about Barney* is about a cat named Barney who died. The book is about life, death, and remembering. Told by the child who was the cat's owner, the book begins, "My cat Barney died last Friday. I was very sad."

Stories are so important to your toddler that even her new picture books will stand or fall on their stories. In looking at wordless storybooks, you will find that the best ones have illustrations so well-conceived and drawn that they convey a clear story line. Your preschooler at this stage wants particularly realistic stories, such as Edward Ardizzone's *The Wrong Side of the Bed,* which follows a grouchy child's rough morning;

*Because her Mother Goose book has been read to her since infancy, this preschooler is able to recite the poems from memory. When choosing a Mother Goose anthology, be sure to select one with bright, memorable pictures that will enchant a youngster and make it a favorite for years.*

# Books for Preschoolers (Ages Three to Six Years)

Bang, Molly, *Ten, Nine, Eight.* A girl and her dad count down to bedtime.

Bemelmans, Ludwig, *Madeline.* There are twelve little girls living in an orphanage and the smallest one is Madeline. A classic set in Paris. Other adventures include *Madeline's Rescue; Madeline and the Bad Hat;* and *Madeline's Christmas.*

Cooney, Barbara, *Miss Rumphius.* Miss Rumphius makes the world more beautiful and invites others to think about how they might do the same.

Freeman, Don, *Corduroy.* A winsome bear with a missing button is claimed by a little girl's love.

Gág, Wanda, *Millions of Cats.* Sings a lilting refrain about hundreds of cats, thousands of cats, millions and billions and trillions of cats.

Keats, Ezra Jack, *The Snowy Day.* A youngster plays in the snow to make designs and then takes a snowball into the house to save.

Krauss, Ruth, *The Carrot Seed.* Illustrated by Crockett Johnson. A boy's family tells him his carrot seed will not sprout, but he knows it will. And it does.

Larrick, Nancy (editor). *When The Dark Comes Dancing: A Bedtime Poetry Book.* Illustrated by John Wallner. A splendid anthology.

McCloskey, Robert, *Make Way for Ducklings.* A family of ducks searches for a place to live safely and finds what it is looking for at the pond in the Boston Commons.

Potter, Beatrix, *The Tale of Peter Rabbit.* That beloved rascal, Peter, has a high old time in Mr. McGregor's vegetable garden but then suffers a tummyache and has to drink chamomile tea for supper.

Sendak, Maurice. *Where the Wild Things Are.* An imaginative trip to a land where young Max is in charge of a tribe of smiling monsters. But he decides to return home where someone loves him best of all.

Slobodkina, Esphyr, *Caps for Sale.* A cap salesman has no luck selling his wares, but when he takes a snooze under a tree, a troop of monkeys becomes very interested in his caps.

all ends well, however, with the youngster cuddling on her mother's lap — just like your youngster. A more adventurous picture-read might be *Anno's Journey,* in which Mitsumasa Anno uses sketches and paintings to depict his trek through northern Europe.

Your preschooler will also enjoy a new alphabet book, and he might find especially appealing one whose pictures tell a story as they present the letters. James Stevenson's *Grandpa's Great City Tour* features illustrations telling of a city tour and crowded with an assortment of objects to be picked out and named. *Anno's Alphabet: An Adventure in Imagination* by Mitsumasa Anno features wood-carved letters represented by one large object with many other related objects in the borders of each page.

**Fairy tales and folk tales**

Between four and six years of age is an excellent time for folk and fairy tales, ancient stories whose authorship is lost in the mists of time. Both, say the experts, can involve your youngster in ways that are emotionally beneficial. Such stories transport a child into a fantasy world quite unlike his own and allow him to deal with his subconscious fears. Because the small overcome the large and good overcomes evil, your young one is reassured all will be well in his own life.

Different fairy tales and folk tales require different levels of emotional maturity, however. The motives of characters can be important, for example. Goldilocks breaks the bears' furniture and eats their food not because she is mischievous but because she is naturally inquisitive. That is quite a different thing from the jealousy Cinderella's stepmother and stepsisters feel for her and the sustained hatred the angry queen feels for Snow White. Children appreciate that the resolutions of the problems in fairy tales and folk tales are clear and definitive, with no open or uncertain endings. This matches the child's view of the world at this age.

**The joys of poetry**

Poetry is another important form of traditional children's literature that you will want to consider. The poems written for youngsters often feature children as characters and, even if not, employ language and expressions to which children joyously respond. The wonderful way in which poets play with words, creating action, moods and rhythms, and the way they manipulate sounds will expand your young one's experience with language patterns and pronunciations and encourage him to play with words himself.

Mother Goose is a traditional first step into poetry. With their sounds and rhythms, these grand old verses are certain to appeal to your child. More formal poems for children frequently deal with everyday experiences and often are told from a child's point of view. A. A. Milne and Robert Louis Stevenson both have chronicled children's lives in verse, while Walter de la Mare is noted for his lyrical poetry evocative of the child's fantasy world. Contemporary poets whose work you may wish to consider include Myra Cohn Livingston, Eve Merriam, Lilian Moore, Karla Kuskin, David McCord, Aileen Fisher, John Ciardi, and Gwendolyn Brooks. Ask at bookstores and libraries for their collections, many of which are handsomely illustrated. There are excellent anthologies that contain poems on a single theme; Nancy Larrick has gathered together bedtime poems in *When the Dark Comes Dancing,* and Lee Bennett Hopkins has gathered poems about the world of long ago in *Dinosaurs.*

The best poems for children have a lilting, singsong quality about them. And they are blessedly direct; your child will tune out obscure poems and overlong, heavily descriptive ones. As you and your child embark on the pleasures of poetry, you can help get him started by introducing a poem with a short explanation of what it is about or by posing a question the poem will answer. If a poem has repetitive lines, you might alternate them with your youngster, letting him repeat the line you just spoke. This will give him a real sense of participation and will help in developing his language skills. Better still, it will draw the two of you together, which is, after all, a goal in itself. ❖

# What Makes a Good Picture Book

Picture books play a vital role in your child's development. Yet with thousands to choose from, how should you choose the best ones? Here are five guidelines — qualities found in the work of the foremost illustrators of children's books.

*Accuracy.* The illustrations are faithful to the text, showing scenes and characters as they are described in the story. The red-haired prince always has red hair; the twelve little girls are accounted for in each picture. Youngsters have a way of checking these details, and they are disconcerted when they discover errors. The best illustrators also match the text in mood and style, using a delicate line and subtle palette for an elfin tale, and a bold, flat style for a factual book about trains. And each picture is positioned where it belongs in the text, to be seen while its part of the story is read.

*Imagination.* The illustrations add a dimension to the text, giving youngsters another way to interact with the book and encouraging them to use their imaginations, too. In *Goodnight Moon (below),* the text mentions a "young mouse" in the room, but only in the illustrations does the mouse move about as the story unfolds. Children eagerly look to find the mouse in its new spot as each page is turned.

*Storytelling.* The pictures tell the story coherently and portray all of the important action. A child who has heard the story once or twice can recall all of its essentials just by looking at the illustrations.

*Emotional involvement.* The pictures invite the child into the story, by helping him identify with the characters. Children feel kinship with little animals in their vulnerability; and seeing a picture of a boy trying hard to whistle, a child might say, "I know just how he feels."

*Artistic merit.* The best and most lasting illustrations are artistically sound, showing original, balanced, and harmonious use of line, shape, and texture. Color, though often wonderful, is not essential for enjoyment.

Below and on the following pages is a sampler of marvelous art from classic children's picture books, both old and new.

This illustration by Clement Hurd, in Margaret Wise Brown's *Goodnight Moon,* gives children lots to look at; they love pointing to the things mentioned in the text. Hurd's clear, restful colors capture the soothing warmth of a young rabbit's bedtime ritual.

A curious crow puzzles over a five-pound bank note in this watercolor by Arthur Rackham for J. M. Barrie's *Peter Pan in Kensington Gardens.* A master of realistic detail, Rackham made the fantasy realm of elves, fairies, and bespectacled mice delightfully visible.

Beatrix Potter's naughty bunny savors a pilfered carrot from Mr. McGregor's garden in this watercolor from *The Tale of Peter Rabbit,* published in 1902. Peter seems very real to young children, who admire him for venturing forth but fear for his safety.

The dish runs away with the spoon in this lively cartoon from Randolph Caldecott's 1882 book of nursery rhymes, *Hey Diddle Diddle.* It was Caldecott who introduced spritely action and humor into children's book art; the American Library Association's prestigious Caldecott Medal is named in his honor.

This woodcut from *Baby's Own Aesop* is by Walter Crane, an Englishman who brought unified design and quality printing to children's books in the 1860s. Children today enjoy the formal beauty and the sense of long-ago in Crane's illustrations.

Pupils leave school after their lessons, in a watercolor by Kate Greenaway for her 1879 book of poems, *Under the Window*. Dressed quaintly even for their own day, Greenaway's children have a sweetness that still appeals to youngsters.

Pooh Bear muses over the signs posted at Owl's house in this pen-and-ink drawing by Ernest Shepard for A. A. Milne's *Winnie the Pooh*. Shepard captured each character's personality and endearing foibles in his simple, gently humorous drawings.

A dazzling butterfly emerges from a cocoon on the last page of *The Very Hungry Caterpillar* by Eric Carle. In bright collages of painted rice paper, Carle takes children through the caterpillar's metamorphosis and offers practice in numbers and the days of the week.

Hapless Big Anthony bobs on a tide of magic spaghetti cascading from Grandma Witch's house in *Strega Nona*, an Italian folk story retold and illustrated by Tomie de Paola. The artist's simple style perfectly suits the sturdy old peasant tale.

A burly policeman halts traffic for Mrs. Mallard and her brood in *Make Way for Ducklings* by author-illustrator Robert McCloskey. The umber-and-white drawings perfectly fit the story of a mother duck safely guiding her little ones about in the big world.

A locomotive pouring forth smoke pulls colorful cars across the pages of *Freight Train*, written and illustrated by Donald Crews. The bold, airbrushed pictures give a sense of excitement in presenting information about the world.

Peter tries to whistle for his dog, Willie, but nothing comes out, in Ezra Jack Keats's *Whistle for Willie.* Keats won renewed popularity for the collage medium as he pioneered a black youngster's success story in a popular picture book.

Naughty Max's room begins turning into a forest in Maurice Sendak's *Where the Wild Things Are.* The poetic text and comical pictures let children explore their frightening anger in safety, because triumphant Max is loved, wildness and all.

Twelve little girls in a Parisian convent school form a tooth-brushing squad in Ludwig Bemelmans's *Madeline.* In his tale of the smallest and most spirited pupil, Bemelmans matches his spare, expressive drawings to his whimsical rhymes.

# Spinning Your Own Tales

As important and enjoyable as reading aloud to your child can be, there may come times when you would prefer to tell her a story, perhaps one you have made up, or one chosen from your experiences as an adult or recalled from your childhood. By all means, go right ahead. Unconstrained by someone else's words, you can involve your youngster directly in your tale, with both of you joining in the fantasy you create. With a little planning and practice you will soon be able to hold her spellbound, while she creates images in her mind to illustrate the tale you are telling. And what is so nice about it all is the spontaneity; you are free to tell a story any time — while you are out walking, driving in a car, or just before your youngster's bedtime.

Storytelling engages the heart as well as the mind, and it can be used to help your young one through difficult situations. If she is anxious about going off to nursery school or kindergarten for the first time, try soothing her with an upbeat tale about a little girl entering a strange new place and quickly making friends with all the children there. You can model the main character after your youngster, if that seems right, or you can disguise the character as a doll or animal and still get your message across.

**Some secrets of good storytelling**

To be able to tell a story well you must, of course, enjoy it yourself. Just be sure that the plot is easy to follow so that your child will not lose interest. If you pick a well-known fable or folk tale to retell, you may have to simplify it. But be careful to preserve the basic structure. No story succeeds better than one with a distinct beginning, middle, and end. Obviously you will want to avoid too many digressions and side plots, since these distract and confuse a young listener. After setting the scene and introducing the characters, take pains to develop the situation or conflict interestingly, and then resolve it happily at the end.

The best stories invariably have characters with endearing qualities — perhaps a Teddy bear that can talk — or strong and colorful personalities. They also contain plenty of action. Even very young children can be swept along by the dramatic events you recount, so long as they involve lots of repetition of words and sounds and are not too frightening. Older children love suspense. Choose evocative words that awaken the senses. A well-told tale rich in sensory images will make your child believe that she can smell the hay as you describe a little girl like herself running barefoot through a newly mown field, chasing a yellow butterfly.

*A youngster pretends he is a Billy Goat Gruff in the well-known tale, while his father, acting out the part of the troll, growls, "Who's that tripping over my bridge?" Children love dramatizations of stories that use simple props such as this table bridge and homemade mask.*

Taking all these elements into account, cast your story to fit the age level and interests of your youngster. An easy way to gauge the suitability of its plot and language is to browse through her favorite books. As for length, restrict it to her attention span. While some children pay attention for only ten minutes, others will listen for half an hour. The well-told story — short or long — will leave your youngster satisfied, and when you tell it at bedtime, it will float around in her mind after you have finished, turning slowly into dreams.

**Sources for storytellers**  Some parents feel uncomfortable about inventing a story of their own. But do not let that stop you from storytelling. One way to proceed is to select a classic fairy tale, such as "Little Red Riding Hood," and relate it in your own words, with all the enthusiasm you can muster. The anthologies at your library will be full of appropriate stories. An especially good collection of folk tales, myths, and fantasy is *The Arbuthnot Anthology of Children's Literature* by May Hill Arbuthnot. You will also find many books on how to be a good storyteller. Among the best is *Storytelling: Art & Technique* by Ellin Greene and Augusta Baker.

If you want to be more original, adapt a well-known favorite such as "Snow White and the Seven Dwarfs" and put your child into it as one of the central characters. Or you can make up an amusing title that will intrigue your youngster, such as "The Cat Who Couldn't Meow," and then weave a story around it. You can also draw upon events past, present, or future in her life and base your yarn on them. If you are planning a family vacation, create an adventure about a family on holiday. It will fill her with happy anticipation for the trip to come.

Some of the best stories to spin are those based on your own childhood. Children love to hear parents tell about themselves when they were children. Think, too, of the stories told to you by your own parents or grandparents — especially the fascinating ones that described what life was like long ago. Youngsters treasure these stories, and when they become adults, they will pass them on to the next generation in the true oral tradition of our forebears.

**Preparing the tale and delivering it**

Once you have decided on a story, take sufficient time to prepare yourself. Think about how you might enhance your delivery to hold your child's attention. As you tell your story, modulate your voice, using different pitches to convey various moods or to suit a character. You can also vary your pace — speeding up or slowing down to create an effect. Pauses can be used to signal a dramatic turn. Appropriate gestures will enhance the drama further, such as stretching out your arms as far they can go when you describe a giant. But be careful not to overdo it, or you may divert your youngster from what you are saying.

You will get better with each story you tell, especially if you watch your little one's reactions and learn from them. Take encouragement from the fact that many famous books began as stories made up on the spot to entertain children, among them *Alice in Wonderland* and *Winnie the Pooh.*

**Building on the experience**

Storytelling serves not only to stretch your youngster's imagination, deepen her thought processes, and provide her with insights, but also to nurture future reading skills by enriching her vocabulary and teaching her story structure. With this in mind, encourage your youngster to repeat refrains or key phrases, or even let her play one of the characters. After you have told her "Goldilocks" two or three times, pause on the next telling for a second before the refrain, "Who's been eating my porridge?" and wait for her to join in. Chances are she will do so eagerly.

You can increase the value of storytelling by initiating a discussion afterward. If your tale has involved animals, ask questions about their sizes, shapes, and colors. Have some picture books ready to show. You might even suggest an excursion to the zoo or a farm. And always listen to and respond to the questions or comments your child has for you.

You may want to use props to add excitement to the tale or to draw out your child *(pages 115-117).* Some storytellers employ flannel boards — stiff, felt-covered surfaces on which they stick felt cutouts of characters and objects — to illustrate their tales. Dramatizing a story with puppets or masks is a particularly good way to engage a youngster who may be shy. Whatever you do, and however you tell your story, the payoff is bound always to be the same — a shared moment of closeness and love. ⋰

# Adding a Colorful Dimension

From time to time, you may want to add an extra dimension to your storytime routine by using simple homemade props, such as hand or finger puppets, or perhaps a hand shadow on the wall *(right)*. The props will help your youngster experience literature in a way that can be more interesting than simply listening. What is more, making the props can be fun for you and your little one; all you need are a few art supplies, some common household items, and a little creativity.

As your youngster manipulates a puppet or a hand shadow, she can pantomime a character's actions or even create her own dialogue and tell the story herself. Your presence as an appreciative audience may be all the encouragement she will need. As she performs, she will experience the character's plight and share its thoughts, motivations, and feelings — all of which helps her to grow as a perceptive reader.

Stories that lend themselves to dramatization are short, with few characters, few scenes, and lots of action. Mother Goose rhymes and the fairy-tale classics are excellent sources.

**Paper-Plate Masks**
*Hidden behind a paper-plate mask, your child can shed her inhibitions and act out the role of a character from a favorite story — in this case, "The Three Little Pigs." If she is old enough, have her cut out the faces from construction paper, using safety scissors, and glue them and the wooden tongue-depressor handles onto the plates. Let her draw on the features of the animals with a black felt-tip marker.*

**Shadow Dramatics**
*By casting hand shadows on the wall, you can make an animal spring to life in your child's room. For this rabbit, raise the first two fingers of the right hand and touch the last two together (top). Then, curl the first two fingers of the left hand, straighten the thumb, and extend the third and fourth fingers (center), so they can be grasped by the thumb and last two fingers of the right hand (bottom).*

## Paper-Bag Puppets

*With a little artwork, you can transform lunch-size paper bags into enchanting storybook characters — here, Goldilocks and the Three Bears. Draw each character so that the bottom of the bag bisects its mouth. By placing the fingers in the bottom of the bag and using the thumb as a lever, you can make the puppet talk.*

## Cutouts for Little Fingers

*Action-packed nursery rhymes such as "Three Blind Mice" or fables such as "The Tortoise and the Hare" lend themselves to finger puppets. The puppets can be drawn freehand or traced from a book and cut out. One version is taped around the child's finger; the other kind has holes cut so that little fingers become the puppet's legs.*

## Making Stick Puppets

*In a child's hand, stick puppets such as these illustrating "Little Red Riding Hood" can be made to hop, glide, or pounce. The base of each one is a picture traced from a book, cut out of construction paper, and then glued onto a tongue depressor or ice-pop stick. Stick puppets are well-suited for tales with lots of characters.*

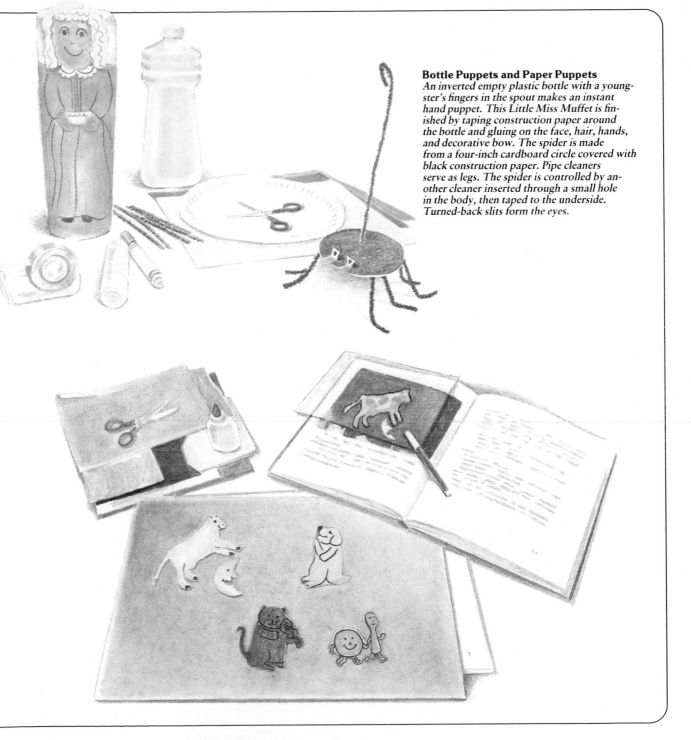

**Bottle Puppets and Paper Puppets**
*An inverted empty plastic bottle with a young-ster's fingers in the spout makes an instant hand puppet. This Little Miss Muffet is fin-ished by taping construction paper around the bottle and gluing on the face, hair, hands, and decorative bow. The spider is made from a four-inch cardboard circle covered with black construction paper. Pipe cleaners serve as legs. The spider is controlled by an-other cleaner inserted through a small hole in the body, then taped to the underside. Turned-back slits form the eyes.*

**A Display Board of Felt**
*This flannel board displaying characters from the nursery rhyme "Hey Diddle Diddle" is made by gluing a rectangular piece of colored felt onto a similar-size piece of poster board. The characters are also of felt. Use tracing paper to make templates for them. Because felt is difficult to cut with safety scissors, you may need to do the cutting. Add detail with a black felt-tip pen.*

# 5 School Days

The two gleeful kindergartners opposite are clearly looking forward to the school day ahead. And why not? In the next few hours, they will be learning quite a lot about reading, and that makes them feel rather proud and very important.

Such excitement in learning is what all parents wish for their youngsters, and if you have made reading a happy and meaningful part of your child's home life, you have already laid a solid foundation for success. But now that she has reached school age, you will want to know how her teachers plan to carry on the good work.

Most kindergartners spend their first year in a reading-readiness program that will prepare them for more formal reading instruction in the first grade. During the year they will be tested from time to time to find out what they know and to give the teacher an insight into how they might perform in the future.

Teaching reading is a constantly evolving process and different schools may use different methods. Some still make reading a focused project in both kindergarten and first grade, with specific periods of instruction; others are finding ways to engage children in literacy-building activities throughout the school day.

In kindergartens that take the newer approach to reading-readiness, the highly structured classroom atmosphere is gone; in its place is a scene that looks like a scholastic three-ring circus. In one corner, children huddle in the reading nook; in another, they pore over workbooks; elsewhere, youngsters write at computer terminals or play see-and-hear games with the teacher. Everyone is chattering animatedly.

Some of these children will be introduced to formal reading instruction soon; most will wait perhaps until the first grade to encounter the teaching programs described on pages 128-133. Whenever the time comes, say educators, this whole-language method is so creative that for many children, getting there is half the fun.

# A Head Start

"Reading Is Fundamental," announces the slogan of a nation-wide literacy campaign. And so it is. But fundamental to whom? Fundamental when? Until recently, it certainly was not fundamental to kindergarten. That first year of formal schooling traditionally was reserved for nudging children gently out of the home and into the classroom. Kindergarten was a time for play and for making friends, not for the three R's. But much has changed in our perception of what kindergartners are capable of learning.

For one thing, many children now spend anywhere from one to five years in day-care centers and nursery schools before kindergarten. The result of this schoollike atmosphere, along with early viewing of such educational television programs as "Sesame Street" and "The Electric Company," is that substantial numbers of youngsters arrive at kindergarten already knowing quite a bit about letters, words, and stories. They are fully ready to start in on remarkably interesting reading programs.

The specific instruction varies from school to school, depending on the philosophy toward early reading. However, you can generally count on your little one learning the names of letters and the sounds related to those names. She will be expected to write her name and pick out differences among colors and shapes. And in many kindergartens, literacy training goes well beyond those skills.

To appreciate the effect of this early learning and how it might relate to your efforts to promote reading at home, you should consider how attitudes toward reading instruction have changed over the years. At the center of it all is a concept called "reading readiness," which has to do with the ability of children to benefit from formal reading instruction. As employed today, the phrase means something entirely different from its original use, more than sixty years ago. And there is little indication that the concept will not continue to evolve.

**Changing notions of readiness**

In the 1920s and 30s, educators argued that reading should not and could not be taught to children until they had reached what was called "the teachable moment." That moment came at about six-and-a-half years of age — when children were thought to be neurologically ready, with all their mental, visual, and auditory faculties sufficiently matured to meet the challenges of reading. Educators of that era — continuing right into the 1960s and 70s — considered reading readiness purely a level of cognitive maturity. Once a child reached that level, he had only to be given a few fundamentals to succeed; to begin instruction earlier, on the other hand, was considered potentially harmful.

It is obviously true that no youngster will get very far with reading unless he is ready to learn. But why were children considered unready to read until six-and-a-half? The answer is that theorists of the day equated learning to read with physical advances such as walking and running. This was a reasonable, but faulty comparison. Unlike walking and other physical activities, reading does not take place spontaneously. Children must be taught. However, in the 1960s and 70s, educators increasingly realized that they did not have to wait for a certain level of cognitive maturity to introduce reading and writing to youngsters. It became clear that cognitive maturity is only one part of the equation and that breadth of experience and the innate desire for independent learning are equally important.

Educators and reading theorists formulated exercises and teaching techniques that would strengthen a kindergartner's basic abilities in areas related to reading. They focused on such skills as letter naming, letter-sound matching and the ability to discriminate among shapes, sounds and colors. Over time, a new skills-building approach to reading instruction was refined and formalized into curricula for kindergarten. Such programs came into widespread use and today are the norm in schools throughout the United States.

**The skills-building approach**

In a skills-building program, the teacher introduces children to a prescribed sequence of exercises. The range of exercises depends on the kindergarten, but it always includes activities to

*This hands-on look at sea shells and starfish may be a first for some of these youngsters. Such show-and-tell activities help prepare them for reading by extending their vocabularies and expanding their range of personal experience. Words first made familiar in speech are easier for children to learn later in print form.*

help youngsters learn the names of the letters, help them match letters with sounds, and help them expand their vocabularies. Usually, there are additional exercises that concentrate on visual perception. There may be games in which the students match similar pictures or find differences in similar pictures. Still other exercises focus on comprehension skills, such as making mental connections between pictures and ideas. Others are devoted to improving auditory discrimination, training the child's ear to hear the differences between single sounds, blended sounds, and whole words. Another listening skill that is singled out is the ability to discern the story line in a narrative. And often there will be specific exercises for improving the child's memory for sequences of sounds, words, and ideas.

Generally, these exercises are presented in workbooks or on worksheets. The teaching materials are developed by the same publishing companies that produce the reading books that are used in the school's first grade. Thus, your child is not only getting practice in specific skill areas, she is becoming familiar with the overall approach to reading that she will use again as she grows older.

**A continuing evolution**

In recent years, many specialists in the field have begun to move away from the heavy emphasis on isolated skills. The new theory holds that children best learn to read by reading itself, and that the kindergarten teacher's job is to keep children as involved as possible in the actual process of reading, right from the beginning. The teacher has to regard reading-readiness instruction as an extension of the language-learning process that has already commenced at infancy in each child.

Interestingly, the teacher operating within this framework usually conducts day-to-day classes in much the same gentle, informal fashion as teachers in an earlier time, when maturity was thought to be the decisive issue in determining reading readiness. Children still finger-paint, build with blocks, model with clay, and listen to stories read by the kindergarten teacher. All of these activities enrich a child's experience and are worthwhile. Various features are added to that tradition, however, in hopes of enhancing and building on the oral skills that kindergartners have already begun to master. More time is spent handling books — learning to hold them right side up and to "read" or look at them from front to back, starting at the top of the page and proceeding to the bottom. Some of this may be old hat to children who have been read to frequently at home, but it is wonderfully new to those who are not so well prepared.

Writing is also much more strongly emphasized, with activities that are aimed not at the technical aspects of handwriting but at developing early self-expression. Moreover, kindergartners are encouraged to learn whole words through constant exposure to words in the daily classroom environment. The youngsters' names may be posted prominently by the hooks in the cloakroom, and on displays of their art work and crafts. Words like "table," "desk," "wall," and "floor" may be affixed to the objects they denote. The teacher may also introduce games of rhyming and alliteration to make children more aware of the sounds they are hearing. The overall tone of reading instruction is nonassertive. Only those who are ready to advance do so, and always on their own initiative.

*On this page from a typical reading-readiness workbook, students are asked to circle items beginning with the "buh" sound of the letter "b." Correct answers include "boy," "bear," "bird," "belt" and, "buttons." Many of the exercises in such books are designed to help children recognize the sounds that make up words.*

**Knowing how your child fits in**

Soon after your child enters kindergarten, if not before, you will probably be invited to an orientation program, at which time the school will present its teaching philosophy and outline learning goals for the year. This is an excellent time to find out all you can about the school's approach to reading readiness. It is also an opportunity to acquaint the teacher with your child's current level of interest in letters, words, sounds, and reading.

The critical question is how your child fits in as a reader compared with the other children in the class. All teachers face the problem of bringing all of their students to some basic level of literacy by the end of the school year, despite differences in their abilities. And a kindergarten class will include children who are highly advanced as readers along with others who have barely begun. If you feel that more is being expected of your youngster than he can comfortably handle — or that he lacks challenge — you should seek an early conference with the teacher to find out how you can supplement classroom work. Very possibly, your close involvement can make the difference between a so-so first year and a memorable one for your child. ❖

# Assessing Reading Readiness

Since most educators agree that children should not start formal reading programs until they are fully ready, it is important for schools to have efficient, objective ways to assess each youngster's preparedness. Tests for that purpose first appeared in the 1930s and are now administered by virtually every school. Though not without their problems, these standardized tests fulfill their stated purposes reasonably well. They are a fairly reliable indicator of whether your child is likely to succeed in formal reading instruction in first grade. They also help the schools track their own success in preparing children for this critical step in the educational process.

**The typical reading-readiness test**

There are numerous competing reading-readiness tests, and although each of them has its biases, they are actually more alike than they are different. The reason is that they all are frequently revised on the basis of their performance. If, for example, the majority of boys and girls who do well on test sections that relate to letter recognition later develop into fluent readers, the test designers conclude that good performance in that area is a valid indicator of reading readiness and they place emphasis on it as they revise tests.

The typical test comes in two versions. Many schools administer a short test early or at midyear in kindergarten to gain a rough idea of a child's skill level. The second test comes at the end of kindergarten or the beginning of first grade. It is somewhat longer and examines a broader range of skills: auditory memory, the ability to recognize beginning consonants of words, letter recognition, shape matching, vocabulary comprehension, and concepts of number and size. For sample questions, see the box on page 125.

A reading-readiness test may be one of several tests your child is given. It is not to be confused with the Wechsler Pre-School and Primary Scale of Intelligence Test, or WPPSI, the most widely administered IQ test for children aged four through six-and-a-half. IQ tests measure cognitive ability, not readiness for reading. Some schools also give developmental screening tests, which focus on learning potential, and dynamic assessment tests, which measure learning speed. Others devise their own screening tests for incoming kindergartners or first-graders. Though these tests sometimes touch upon elements of reading, they are not necessarily valid measures of reading readiness.

**What skills are tested**

The premise of reading-readiness tests is that certain skills, particularly those associated with the ability to discriminate

# What Is on a Typical Test?

What is your child asked to do when she takes a reading-readiness test? The sample test items below, adapted from a standardized, nationally marketed reading-readiness test, should give you an idea of the kinds of tasks she will be asked to perform.

Tests may be given in prekindergarten, kindergarten, and first grade. The children taking them are divided into small groups and tested over several days, in subtest sessions that last approximately fifteen minutes. Each subtest measures one skill that is believed to be necessary for successful reading.

Because of their age and inability to read instructions, the children begin with a practice block. Once they know what to expect, they move on to the test itself, with the teacher reading aloud the set of instructions under the actual blocks.

Considered as a whole, a readiness test is just that: a gauge of readiness. It should not be seen as an intelligence test but simply as an indicator of how far along your youngster is on the path toward learning to read.

### School language and listening

*"Circle the picture that shows 'The rabbit is near the tree.'" Test items like this one measure mastery of certain abstract concepts — such as near, below, between, none, some, last, and smallest — that are needed for, among other things, following teachers' directions. These basic language concepts are also very important for the child's later reading comprehension, as well as for solving problems that call for identifying attributes or for comparing, classifying, or sequencing things.*

### Letter recognition

*"In this row, circle the m." Educators agree that being able to identify the letters is a good predictor of a youngster's reading achievement in later years. By itself, however, letter recognition does not constitute reading readiness; if a child fails to recognize the letters, merely giving her exercises that drill her with the letters will not succeed in making her ready to read.*

### Visual matching

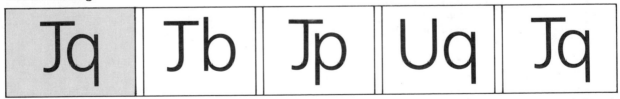

*"Look at what is in the shaded box. Then look carefully at the other boxes in this row. Circle the box that has the same thing in it as the shaded box has. Mark the one that is just like it, the one that matches it." Being able to distinguish between very similar shapes is crucial for discerning the difference between "ball" and "tall" on a printed page. Auditory discrimination, the ability to recognize distinguishing characteristics among sounds, is also crucial and is tested separately.*

### Auditory memory

*"Mark the box that shows the things that I will name. Close your eyes and listen. Right after I say the words, open your eyes and mark the right answer. DOG . . . STAR . . . KEY . . . FORK."*

*Auditory memory is the ability to remember a heard sequence and pick the matching visual (left-to-right) sequence. This is important in reading, writing, and listening, for it is not enough to know what sounds are represented — the young reader has to know their order, so as to distinguish between "bat" and "tab."*

sounds, must be developed before a child can begin to read. The tests seek to assess how many of those skills have already been acquired. In theory, teachers and school administrators can then plan curriculum needs around the test scores, knowing how many relatively advanced pupils they have and how many children they have who are still in need of prereading work. The scores can also help to divide classes into well-matched reading groups.

In practice, however, schools tend to be highly idiosyncratic in their use of test scores. For the most part, the scores seem not to play a significant role in curriculum planning. More often, they are used to make decisions about individual students — chiefly, whether to move a youngster along to first grade, to retain him in kindergarten, or supply remedial help.

**Scoring procedures**

After your youngster has been tested, you will receive a report of her scores, and you may be invited to discuss them in person. The test scores generally are ranked by what is called "norm-reference." This means that the score rates your child's reading skill development against the performance of a large number of children who have taken the test at the identical point in their schooling. One of the most widely used tests, for example, is based on a nationwide sample of 100,000 children. In simplest terms, norm-referencing tells you how your child's reading skill development compares with that of other children his age.

Norm-referenced scores can be expressed in terms of a grade equivalent: If your youngster receives a grade equivalent of 1.6 when tested in the sixth month of first grade, she has scored what is estimated to be average for a child at that time. But such scoring can be misleading to some parents and most experts prefer other methods of ranking test performance. Test results may be rendered, for instance, by percentiles. If your child scores in the seventy-fifth percentile, she has done better than 75 percent of her peers and worse than 25 percent. A third way to rate performance is by stanines, which render scores on a scale of one to nine, with five representing an average performance. A stanine of nine is very high, a one is very low. The percentile rank is determined by comparing a student's score to the national sample. The stanine ranking is used to rank students in the same class or same grade in the local school system.

**How the tests are administered**

Typically, teachers give the longer test in six fifteen-minute sessions, spread over six school days. So that teachers can supervise closely, no more than fifteen children are tested together. A practice session is conducted a day or two before the test begins, and youngsters who have difficulty with the process are given extra practice. The basic procedure is for the teacher to read aloud and repeat each of the questions in each session. The children answer by marking the picture, number, or letter they select on their answer sheets *(box, page 125).*

In some cases, the tests are corrected by the publishers and returned to the school. More often, however, they are graded by the teacher, who may or may not add an informal assessment of the child's reading abilities. And sometimes a teacher may decide that a particular child is ready to read, poor test performance notwithstanding.

**A swirl of controversy** Despite all the research that has gone into them, reading-readiness tests are subject to considerable controversy. The problem, critics say, lies not so much in the tests themselves but in the drawing of too many conclusions from the results. The tests are designed to be predictors of readiness for reading instruction, not to be indicators of current or future overall learning potential. There are far too many variables at work to rely on reading scores for that.

Moreover, some youngsters, who may be fully ready for reading instruction, are not good at taking tests. Some become overly anxious. Others tire too quickly, have inadequate attention spans, or simply do not feel tip-top the week of the test. A number of children fare badly because they come from homes in which reading and writing are neglected. Still others have strengths that are not revealed by standardized tests — intellectual curiosity, for one thing. They may well become excellent readers despite low test scores. And some children develop in such fits and starts that they may lag behind the norm during one test only to leap far ahead scarcely a month later.

Critics also argue that schools are slow in adapting to advances in the science of testing. Many schools continue to use tests that are no longer up-to-date. As a result, children may be held back in school on the basis of incorrect data. As a parent, you may not be qualified to determine the merits of the tests your child takes, but you certainly can take a good hard look at how they are used. And you have every right to challenge test scores that differ sharply from your own knowledge of your child's abilities. When in doubt, talk to the school principal. If you are still not satisfied with your child's evaluation, by all means arrange to have your youngster retested, either at his own school or someplace else. ⬦

# When Formal Instruction Begins

Formal reading instruction, whether it begins late in the kindergarten year or some weeks into first grade, is at the heart of elementary school education. Nothing else that happens in the classroom comes close to having as great a long-term impact. It is hardly surprising, then, that there has always been debate over how literacy should be taught. Many approaches have been tried in modern years. Two of the earliest and best — phonics and whole-word instruction — continue to be used today. The phonics approach teaches children letter and sound correspondences, which permit them to sound out the words they see on a page. Whole-word instruction tries to get children started reading more quickly by teaching them to recognize a small number of frequently used words. Two other methods — called language-experience and whole-language instruction — have gained considerable currency in recent years. A teacher using the language-experience method transcribes the stories her students tell her, which they then read together. The whole-language approach immerses children in print with free and directed reading and writing, as well as many other activities.

However, most educators today believe that no single teaching strategy is entirely adequate. Reading curricula that combine various methods have become the rule, and the mix that prevails these days is phonics and whole-word teaching.

In practical terms, what you are likely to find in your child's classroom is a preplanned, packaged curriculum developed by one of a dozen or more large educational publishing houses. The publisher will provide all the necessary teacher guides, workbooks, textbooks, and audiovisual materials. Often, the same reading curriculum will be in use throughout an entire school system.

*The page below is from a phonics workbook used to augment the day-to-day reading lessons of first-graders. This exercise involves picking out initial consonant sounds and circling the letters that correspond to those sounds. Generally, children practice phonics in conjunction with readings in a primer.*

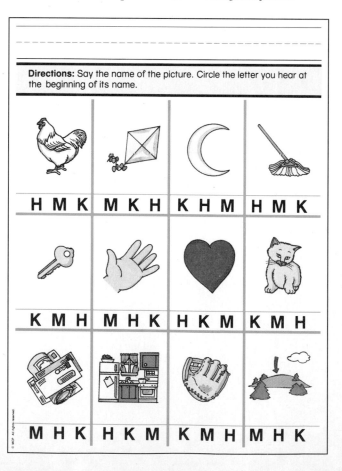

**Directions:** Say the name of the picture. Circle the letter you hear at the beginning of its name.

|  |  |  |  |
|---|---|---|---|
| H M K | M K H | K H M | H M K |
| K M H | M H K | H K M | K M H |
| M H K | H K M | K M H | M H K |

**The phonics method**

The basic tools of phonics instruction are the ABC's, the shapes of the letters, and their sounds. Phonics typically builds on the letter recognition that has already begun in reading-readiness programs. Focusing on one letter at a time, often for several days, the teacher draws the child's attention to the sound — or phoneme — and the shape of each letter. For the majority of the consonants, there is a simple relationship between the sound and the letter. The letter *b*, for example, sounds the same in *ball, bat, butter,* and *Billy.* But a few consonants have two or more phonemic possibilities. For example, the letter *c* paired with the letter *a* in *car* has a hard *k* sound; but *c* paired with *e* in *cell* takes a soft *s* sound. The vowels present similarly confusing ranges of sound. A child will eventually have to learn all the ways the twenty-six letters of the alphabet can be combined to produce the forty-four distinct phonemes of the English language.

In the beginning weeks of phonics instruction, students are guided to concern themselves chiefly with the initial letters of words, because these are easiest to hear and see. As they become better versed in letter recognition, usually about the middle of first grade, they are given more challenging problems, and the featured sounds turn up at the ends or in the middle of words. When students get to the letter *n,* for example, they are drilled in hearing and seeing it in *new* and in *man.* In a typical phonics program, children graduate from first grade having been formally introduced to virtually all of the single consonant sounds. They have also encountered some sounds produced by letter combinations, such as *bl, sp, sh,* and *wh.* And they know the five short vowel sounds for *a, e, i, o,* and *u.* The teaching of phonics will continue until the end of second or third grade, but the emphasis placed on it becomes less and less as time goes by.

*The stories in a primer are exceedingly simple, but they describe events that are both real and understandable to small children. The idea of a dog swimming to fetch a ball, for example, may be quite compelling to a first-grader. The new word on this page is "lake." It is set off by a small illustration to make it easier and more fun to learn.*

The dog sees Matt.

The dog sees the ball.

The dog runs into the

big  lake  .

Will the dog swim to the ball?

## The Purpose of a Basal Reader

At the core of almost every American elementary school's reading program is a basal-reader series or program. Designed to teach the basal, or fundamental, reading skills, a basal-reader program also has important social goals. It should inspire a high regard for reading and its rewards, and it should serve as a vessel of culture, showing children our rich literary heritage and the great diversity of our society.

The program centers on a reader, or in the early grades, pre-primers and primers — anthologies of readings that provide sequential skills building. Each reader has its own workbooks and skills-practice sheets; teachers' manuals give instructions and offer ideas for planning and enriching the lessons.

In a typical kindergarten reading-readiness lesson, youngsters practice such skills as recognizing letters, finding shapes that match, finding a sequence of pictures the teacher has named, and picking out the picture whose name starts with a given sound. If your child has enjoyed storytimes at home and at the library, these exercises may not seem much like reading to her; she knows that reading involves words and stories. You can help her come to grips with this seeming contradiction by continuing to read to her and pointing out rhyming words or words that begin with the same sounds. Do the same with simple or favorite words; remember that the concrete words and the action words — the nouns and verbs — are the words children learn most easily.

There is some debate over the effectiveness of basal-reader-programs. Supporters point to the systematic practice a basal series provides in the skills that build reading proficiency; and the programs give children a wealth of practice with the thousand or so words that constitute most of our everyday communication. Critics argue that the anthology selections, each prefaced by a "Vocabulary Study," make reading artificially easy; after all, no newspaper article defines its "hard words" in a special section at the beginning. At the same time, they say, simplifying the vocabulary of a classic story robs it of complexity and interest — the very things that would motivate a youngster to learn the unfamiliar words.

On balance, it seems clear that a basal-reader series can teach a child basic reading skills. It certainly should not be her only experience of reading, however.

The advantage of starting reading instruction with phonics is that it gives a youngster a tool with which to puzzle out the sounds of words that are unfamiliar. Increasingly, after first grade, he will come across many words that he has never seen before in his life. The chief disadvantage is that phonics is daunting to many children, particularly those who have not been exposed to much reading or do not hear much conversation in their homes. The relationships between the sounds and the shapes of the letters have to be learned by rote, and it is understandable that many children have a hard time maintaining an interest. Some youngsters have been known to end up going through the motions of repeating sounds without ever learning how to apply those sounds to words. Phonics also does nothing by itself to teach reading comprehension. Some critics even argue that phonics distracts children from the basic purpose of reading, which is to find meaning in printed words. It is for these reasons that phonics instruction is typically paired with one of the other word- and idea-oriented teaching methods right from the very beginning.

**The whole-word approach**

At various times, the whole-word approach to reading instruction has been called sight-recognition and look-say reading. Its aim is to take advantage of a youngster's natural ability to remember words. As many parents know, children as young as three or four can learn to read their own names — merely because of interest and frequent exposure. What they have learned is not the actual spellings of words but their visual images or shapes, much in the way they learn to recognize the faces of friends and family members.

The virtue of whole-word instruction from a young child's point of view is that she can learn to read meaningful words, sentences, even whole stories, before she has learned to sound out words letter by letter. She thus begins to understand that ideas and stories are communicated through reading. Moreover, if your youngster is inclined to read for pleasure on her own, she will be able to expand her vocabulary more rapidly, and this accelerates learning all the more. Whole-word reading also gives children a better feel for what reading will eventually become. Mature readers do not look at words letter by letter; they do not even look at individual words but take in entire phrases and sentences at a glance.

Whole-word instruction relies heavily on the use of basal primers and readers *(box, opposite).* In first grade, the children usually work from booklets called preprimers or primers before they move on to the actual readers. For whole-word instruction, the stories in these books are written from a list of basic words that appear very frequently in children's stories and conversations. The various first-grade materials differ somewhat in the words they choose to target for sight-memorization, but a typical example contains 220 different words. These 220 words represent 65 to 70 percent of the vocabulary that first-graders will come across in all their reading wherever they may find themselves outside the classroom. The primers introduce new words, a few at a time. Each new word is repeated several times when it is first presented. As students work their way through the preprimers and primer, recognizing more and more words on sight, the reading selections steadily become more challenging for them. Sentences become longer, the number of characters in stories increases, and the plot or message of the stories becomes more complex.

**The language-experience approach**

While whole-word instruction emphasizes individual words, the language-experience approach looks at all the different ways children use language and tries to find meaningful purposes for language within the classroom setting. In a typical exercise, the teacher asks the children to make up a story about real events in their lives or ones they create out of their imagination and writes down their words as they tell their stories. When the students are asked to read back the story, they have a head start on decoding the writing because the story is their own invention. In some ways, this approach is like whole-word instruction without the constraints imposed by a basal reader. Advocates of the language-experience method contend that their approach revolves more directly around the needs and interests of individual children than the phonics or whole-word teaching method does. The language-experience approach encourages children to perceive reading and writing as simply two more ways to communicate. They soon understand that these tools of communication are no more formidable than talking or listening.

Little concern is given to the order in which particular skills are mastered. The presumption is that a youngster will either ask for help or sort out the problem on her own. The reading vocabulary she learns is drawn mainly from the vocabulary she uses in everyday speech. And the story situations that come up in class are familiar and therefore meaningful to her. Children also are encouraged to write their own labels, notes, and stories as they find they need them. They may even try to write before they have the ability to produce intelligible sentences. In the meantime, the teacher is making certain that the children are surrounded by books and other reading materials that reflect the interests and experiences of the individual students. The premise in choosing these books is that children learn best when they are acquainted with and interested in the subject matter. Children are encouraged, however, to take up easy books at first and only later to attempt more challenging reading.

*Taking dictation from the children, this teacher builds a reading lesson around the words and ideas of her students. Such exercises — in which language is put to practical use — typify an approach to reading instruction called the language-experience method.*

In the 1960s and 70s, when language-experience instruction was still very new, it was heralded for turning some children into avid readers at an early age. But it also put extraordinary demands on the teachers, who had to develop their own classroom materials and activities to suit the needs of several groups in the same class. Often actual classroom performance failed to measure up to expectations. Because the program was difficult to sustain, the language-experience approach to reading has been expanded into the broader, more effective whole-language method.

**The whole-language approach**

A kindergarten class involved in the whole-language process is depicted in the essay beginning on page 134. The method seeks to create a happy blend of the best features of phonics, whole-word, and language-experience, with children in a classroom setting that is literally surrounded by examples of the language arts.

The program teaches children to read with four goals kept in mind. The first is to help children recognize that written language can be of great service to them. A second aim is to help children understand the characteristics of printed words. A third goal is to demonstrate the need for writing to be both consistent and explicit, in order to be understood by others. The final goal is to assist youngsters to develop a positive attitude toward printed words.

In the first year of a whole-language program, students spend roughly equal amounts of time reading, writing, speaking, and listening. Within the many and varied classroom projects, these activities are treated not as separate entities but as closely related communications skills. In the beginning, while children's reading skills are still very limited, the teacher offers materials known as "predictable language books." Sources such as "This is the House that Jack Built," or "The Three Bears," use repetition and predictability of sequence to allow children to read along with their teacher and at times even attempt to read all by themselves. As the school year progresses and their communications skills continue to improve, students are exposed to ever more varied books, magazines, and other printed materials. Always the standard to be maintained is that the reading matter be useful and meaningful to the children. Youngsters thus become motivated by their own self-interest to continue improving their skills and to reach unhesitatingly beyond their limits to read, write, talk, and listen effectively. ❖

# A Child's Garden of Words

The whole-language approach to reading and writing, used increasingly in kindergartens around the country, emphasizes the beauty and importance of the written word. It provides a child with varied opportunities to manipulate written language and encourages her to experiment boldly with letters and words until she feels comfortable using them. In such a kindergarten, work is play.

The whole-language kindergarten interweaves reading, writing, and spelling throughout almost every activity. In this way, a child sees them as a vital part of everything she does.

Wherever the youngster gazes — at walls, desks, tables, chalkboards — she sees colorful sign-up sheets, charts, directions, alphabet posters, and children's written handiwork. In accessible niches around the room are books to browse or read when she feels like it.

To inspire her to write, slates, magic markers, pencils, and paper lie scattered about. She may pick them up and try them at her pleasure.

Free though it may seem, the whole-language approach is not without structure. While the teacher lets the children discover many things for themselves, she also reads to them, writes notes addressed to individual pupils, holds discussions, dramatizes stories, and coaches children to write or tell stories in their own words. Through activities she imparts a love of reading and writing that can last a lifetime.

*Having someone read aloud stimulates children's imagination and teaches them that a book yields pleasure as well as information. This teacher might start by discussing a book's structure. Then, as the story progresses, she might ask the children what they think will happen next, thereby sharpening analytical and problem-solving skills.*

I HEAR I FORGET, I SEE I REMEMBER

April

I am at the bathroom

Tommy will feed the 🐟

Melanie will write the 4 6 7

Trae will put up the ☀

Shirleeta will be the 👫👫

Natosha will put up the ▪

Shinita will take up the ✉

LaToya will water the 🪴

Nancy

Please do my our

Please do my our

knock not down

knock not down

Eric
Sophie
Laquita
Stasha
al
rystal

Jacob
Tony
Carrie
Mamie
LaToya
Terasa
Samuel

Since children readily learn their own names, the teacher can integrate names into many activities under the whole-language approach. The girl at left above, for example, is clipping her name on a wheel before leaving the room, while the girl at right above is changing name tags on the schedule of activities. The girl at left below is retrieving something from her drawer, which she identifies by reading her name. And the youngster at right below is stringing words together to make up her own instructions.

Please knock not down

The students at far right are working on a word-search puzzle, hunting for classmates' names in the grid, while the girl next to them is referring to an alphabet tape as she creates a story in her own words. The girl below is writing a story, referring to words commonly used by the children and vowel sounds given by the teacher.

Writing

VOWELS

ă cat    ā table
ĕ tent   ēē see
ĭ sit    Ī kite
ŏ mop    ō toe  OO moon
ŭ puppy  ū tune

Words We Are Learning

Mrs.
is      a       of
the     can     to
it      this    we
that    day     do
in      and     will
for     on      up
        was     not

Listening

One method of teaching children to read is to let them select and listen to taped stories or records while they follow along in their books. They can repeat the words, read along silently or out loud, or choose any other method of listening they enjoy.

The whole-language method stresses the importance of writing something every day — be it a letter, story, or anything else that strikes a child's fancy. To blend reading and writing, a teacher can let willing students read their work aloud, as above, and students' work can also be displayed for all to read silently.

Language comes alive when children are involved in dramatic play. The whole-language approach fosters the use of print during the drama. In this illustration, the boy at left reads the address of the burning house and uses his make-believe radio to dispatch two fire fighters there. Note that the children have invented their own spelling of the address 801 E. Chapman St.

# Bibliography

## BOOKS

Anderson, Gordon S., *A Whole Language Approach to Reading*. Lanham, Md.: University Press of America, 1984.

Anderson, Richard C., Jean Osborne and Robert J. Tierney, *Learning to Read in American Schools: Basal Readers and Content Texts*. Hillsdale, N.J.: Lawrence Erlbaum Associates, 1984.

Auckerman, Robert C., *Approaches to Beginning Reading, Second Edition*. New York: John Wiley & Sons, 1984.

Bader, Barbara, *American Picturebooks: From Noah's Ark to the Beast Within*. New York: Macmillan Publishing Co., 1976.

Bauer, Caroline Feller, *Handbook for Storytellers*. Chicago: American Library Association, 1977.

Boegehold, Betty Doyle, *Getting Ready to Read*. New York: Ballantine Books, 1984.

Breneman, Lucille N. and Bren Breneman, *Once Upon a Time: A Storytelling Handbook*. Chicago: Nelson-Hall, 1983.

Burie, Audrey Ann, and Mary Ann Heltshe, *Reading with a Smile*. Washington, D.C.: Acropolis Books, 1975.

Butler, Dorothy, *Babies Need Books*. New York: Atheneum, 1985.

Butler, Dorothy and Marie Clay, *Reading Begins at Home*. Exeter, New Hampshire: Heinemann Educational Books, 1982.

Cascardi, Andrea E., *Good Books to Grow On*. New York: Warner Books, 1985.

Champlin, Connie, and Nancy Renfro, *Storytelling with Puppets*. Chicago: American Library Association, 1985.

Cianciolo, Patricia, *Illustrations in Children's Books, Second Edition*. Dubuque, Ia.: Wm. C. Brown Company, 1976.

Clay, Marie M., *What Did I Write?* Exeter, New Hampshire: Heinemann Educational Books, 1982.

Commission on Reading, *Becoming a Nation of Readers*. Washington, D.C.: National Institute of Education, U.S. Department of Education, 1985.

Cullinan, Bernice E., with Mary K. Karrer and Arlene M. Pillar, *Literature and the Child*. San Diego, Ca.: Harcourt Brace Jovanovich, 1981.

Cullinan, Bernice E. and Carolyn W. Carmichael, eds., *Literature and Young Children*, Urbana, Ill.: National Council of Teachers of English, 1977.

Dallmann, Martha, Roger L. Rouch, Lynette Y. C. Char and John J. DeBoer, *The Teaching of Reading, Sixth Edition*, New York: Holt, Rinehart and Winston, 1982.

Durkin, Dolores, *Teaching Young Children to Read, Fourth Edition*. Boston: Allyn and Bacon, 1987.

Dzama, Mary Ann, and Robert Gilstrap, *Ready to Read*. New York: John Wiley & Sons, 1983.

Farr, Roger and Robert F. Carey, *Reading: What Can Be Measured?* Newark, Delaware: International Reading Association, 1986.

Ferreiro, Emilia, and Ana Teberosky, *Literacy before Schooling*. Exeter, New Hampshire: Heinemann Educational Books, 1982.

Fiarotta, Phyllis, with Noel Fiarotta, *Sticks & Stones & Ice Cream Cones*. New York: Workman Publishing Company, 1973.

Genishi, Celia, and Anne Haas Dyson, *Language Assessment in the Early Years*. Norwood, N.J.: Ablex Publishing Company, 1984.

Gibson, Eleanor J., and Harry Levin, *The Psychology of Reading*. Cambridge, Mass.: The MIT Press, 1975.

Goelman, Hillel, Antoinette A. Oberg, and Frank Smith, *Awakening to Literacy*. Exeter, N.H.: Heinemann Educational Books, 1982.

Goodwin, William L., and Laura A. Driscoll, *Handbook for Measurement and Evaluation in Early Childhood Education*. San Francisco: Jossey-Bass Inc., 1980.

Greene, Ellin, and Augusta Baker, *Storytelling: Art and Technique*. New York: Bowker, 1977.

Gross, Jacquelyn, *Make Your Child a Lifelong Reader*. Los Angeles: Jeremy P. Tarcher, 1986.

Harris, Larry A., and Carl B. Smith, *Reading Instruction: Diagnostic Teaching in the Classroom*. New York: Macmillan Publishing Co., 1986.

Hildebrand, Verna, *Introduction to Early Childhood Education, 4th Edition*. New York: Macmillan Publishing Company, 1986.

Kettelkamp, Larry, *Shadows*. Urbana, Ill.: William Morrow & Company, 1957.

Lamme, Linda Leonard:
*Growing Up Reading*. Washington, D.C.: Acropolis Books Ltd., 1985.
*Growing Up Writing*. Washington, D.C.: Acropolis Books Ltd., 1984.

Lamme, Linda Leonard, ed., *Learning to Love Literature*. Urbana, Ill.: National Council of Teachers of English, 1981.

Lamme, Linda Leonard, with Vivian Cox, Jane Matanzo and Miken Olson, *Raising Readers: A Guide to Sharing Literature with Young Children*. New York: Walker and Company, 1980.

Lapp, Diane, and James Flood, *Teaching Students to Read*. New York: Macmillan Publishing Company, 1986.

Larrick, Nancy, *A Parent's Guide to Children's Reading, Fifth Edition*. New York: Bantam Books, 1982.

Lorton, Mary Baratta, *Workjobs*. Menlo Park, Ca.: Addison-Wesley Publishing Co., 1972.

Machado, Jeanne M., *Early Childhood Experiences in Language Arts, Third Edition*. Albany, N.Y.: Delmar Publishers, 1985.

McMullan, Kate Hall, *How to Choose Good Books for Kids*. Reading, Ma.: Addison-Wesley Publishing Co., 1984.

Meyer, Susan E., *A Treasury of the Great Children's Book Illustrators*. New York: Harry N. Abrams, 1983.

Muncie, Patricia Tyler, *Complete Book of Illustrated K-3 Alphabet Games and Activities*. West Nyack, N.Y.: Center for Applied Research in Education, 1980.

Ollila, Lloyd O., *The Kindergarten Child and Reading*. Newark, Delaware: International Reading Association, 1977.

Oppenheim, Joanne F., Barbara Brenner and Betty D. Boegehold, *Choosing Books for Kids*. New York: Ballantine Books, 1986.

Pearson, P. David, *Handbook of Reading Research*. New York: Longman, 1984.

Pinnell, Gay Su, *Discovering Language with Children*. Urbana, Illinois: National Council of Teachers of English, 1980.

Resnick, Lauren B., and Phyllis A. Weaver, *Theory and Practice of Early Reading - Volume 2*. Hillsdale, N.J.: Lawrence Erlbaum Associates, 1979.

Rubin, Richard R., and John J. Fisher, III, *Your Preschooler*. New York: Macmillan Publishing Co., 1982.

Sampson, Michael R., *The Pursuit of Literacy: Early Reading and Writing*. Dubuque, Iowa: Kendall/Hunt Publishing Company, 1986.

Scarr, Sandra, Richard A. Weinberg and Ann Levine, *Understanding Development*. San Diego, Ca.: Harcourt Brace Jovanovich, 1986.

Schickedanz, Judith A., *More Than the ABC's: The Early Stages of Reading and Writing*. Washington, D.C.: National Association for the Education of Young Children, 1986.

Schickedanz, Judith A., Mary E. York, Ida Santos Stewart and Doris A. White, *Strategies for Teaching Young Children, Second Edition*. Englewood Cliffs, N.J.: Prentice-Hall, 1983.

Schwartz, Steven, *Measuring Reading Competence*. New York: Plenum Press, 1984.

Smith, Frank, *Reading without Nonsense*. New York: Teachers College Press, 1985.

Spodek, Bernard, *Teaching in the Early Years, Third Edition*. Englewood Cliffs, N.J.: Prentice-Hall, 1985.

Spodek, Bernard, ed., *Today's Kindergarten*. New York: Teachers College Press, 1986.

Stern, Daniel, *The First Relationship: Mother and Infant*. Cambridge, Mass.: Harvard University Press, 1977.

Sutherland, Zena, Dianne L. Monson and May Hill Arbuthnot, *Children and Books, Sixth Edition*. Glenview, Illinois: Scott, Foresman and Company, 1981.

Temple, Charles A., Ruth G. Nathan and Nancy A. Burris, *The Beginnings of Writing*. Boston: Allyn and Bacon, 1982.

Trelease, Jim, *The Read-Aloud Handbook*. New York: Penguin Books, 1985.

Waller, T. Gary, and G. E. Mackinnon, *Reading Research: Advances in Theory and Practice, Volume 1*. New York: Academic Press, 1979.

## PERIODICALS

Elkind, David, "We Can Teach Reading Better." *Today's Education,* November/December, 1975.

Elliott, Sharon, John Nowosad and Phyllis Samuels: " 'Me at School,' 'Me at Home': Using Journals with Preschoolers." *Language Arts,* September 1981.

Geller, Linda Gibson, "Children's Rhymes and Literacy Learning: Making Connections." *Language Arts,* February 1983.

Guthrie, John T., "Preschool Literacy Learning." *The Reading Teacher,* December 1983.

Honig, Alice Sterling, "Language Environments for Young Children." *Young Children,* November 1981.

Isham, Nima, "School Testing: A Special Report." *Child,* March/April 1987.

Kontos, Susan, "What Preschool Children Know about Reading and How They Learn It." *Young Children,* November 1986.

Lehr, Fran, "ERIC/RCS Report: Television Viewing and Reading." *Language Arts,* September 1986.

Meisels, Samuel J., "Uses and Abuses of Developmental Screening and School Readiness Testing." *Young Children,* January 1987.

Roncy, R. Craig, "Background Experience Is the Foundation of Success in Learning to Read." *The Reading Teacher,* November 1984.

Schickedanz, Judith A., and Maureen Sullivan, "Mom, What Does U-F-F Spell?" *Language Arts,* January 1984.

Snow, Catherine E., "Literacy and Language: Relationships during the Preschool Years." *Harvard Educational Review,* May 1985.

Sulzby, Elizabeth, "Children's Emergent Reading of Favorite Storybooks: A Developmental Study." *Reading Research Quarterly,* Summer 1985.

Teale, William H., "Toward a Theory of How Children Learn to Read and Write Naturally." *Language Arts,* September 1982.

Vellutino, Frank R., "Dyslexia." *Scientific American,* March 1987.

## OTHER PUBLICATIONS

"Kindergarten Programs and Practices in Public Schools." Arlington, Va.: Educational Research Service, 1986.

"NAHSA Answers Questions about Otitis Media and Language Development." Rockville, Md.: National Association for Hearing and Speech Action, 1985.

"NAHSA Answers Questions about Child Language." Rockville, Md.: National Association for Hearing and Speech Action, 1985.

Nurss, Joanne R., and Mary E. McGauvran, "Metropolitan Readiness Tests - Level 1." New York: The Psychological Corporation, Harcourt Brace Jovanovich, 1986.

"Reading Is Fun! Tips for Parents of Children Age Birth to 8 Years." Washington, D.C.: Reading is Fundamental, Inc., 1983.

"TV and Reading." Washington, D.C.: Reading Is Fundamental, Inc. 1985.

Smith, Elizabeth A., "Essential Prerequisites for Beginning Reading Instruction: An Historical Review." Washington, D.C.: Educational Resources Information Center, 1986.

## CHILDREN'S BOOKS

*The following works have been mentioned in this volume.*

Ahlberg, Janet and Allan:
*Peek-A-Boo!* New York: Viking, 1981.
*Each Peach Pear Plum.* New York: Viking, 1979.

Alexander, Martha, *Pigs Say Oink: A First Book of Sounds.* New York: Random House, 1981.

Anno, Mitsumasa (illus.):
*Anno's Alphabet: An Adventure in Imagination.* New York: Crowell, 1975.
*Anno's Journey.* New York: Putnam, 1981.

Arbuthnot, May Hill, *The Arbuthnot Anthology of Children's Literature.* Glenview, Ill.: Scott, Foresman, 1953.

Ardizzone, Edward, *The Wrong Side of the Bed.* New York: Doubleday, 1970.

Bang, Molly, *Ten, Nine, Eight.* New York: Greenwillow, 1983.

Barrie, Sir James M., *Peter Pan in Kensington Gardens.* Illustrated by Arthur Rackham. New York: Charles Scribner's Sons, 1907.

Barton, Byron:
*Airplanes.* New York: Crowell, 1986.
*Boats.* New York: Crowell, 1986.
*Trains.* New York: Crowell, 1986.
*Trucks.* New York: Crowell, 1986.

Bemelmans, Ludwig:
*Madeline.* New York: Viking Penguin, 1977.
*Madeline and the Bad Hat.* New York: Penguin, 1977.
*Madeline's Christmas.* New York: Viking, 1985.
*Madeline's Rescue.* New York: Penguin, 1977.

Brown, Margaret Wise, *Goodnight Moon.* Illustrated by Clement Hurd. New York: Harper & Row, 1977.

Bruna, Dick, *My Toys.* New York: Methuen, 1980.

Caldecott, Randolph, *Hey Diddle Diddle.* London: Frederick Warne and Co., 1882.

Campbell, Rod, *Dear Zoo.* New York: Four Winds Press, 1983.

Carle, Eric, *The Very Hungry Caterpillar.* New York: Philomel, 1981.

Carroll, Lewis (Charles Lutwidge Dodgson), *Alice's Adventures in Wonderland.* Illustrated by John Tenniel. New York: Macmillan, 1963.

Chorao, Kay, *The Baby's Lap Book.* New York: E. P. Dutton, 1977.

Cooney, Barbara, *Miss Rumphius.* New York: Viking, 1982.

Crane, Walter (Illus.), *Baby's Own Aesop.* London: Warne, 1887, Bodley Head, 1981.

Crews, Donald, *Freight Train.* New York: Greenwillow, 1978.

De Paola, Tomie:
*Strega Nona.* Englewood Cliffs, N.J.: Prentice-Hall, 1975.
*Tomie de Paola's Mother Goose.* New York: Putnam, 1985.

Flack, Marjorie, *Ask Mr. Bear.* New York: Macmillan, 1958.

Freeman, Don:
*Corduroy.* New York: Viking, 1982.
*Corduroy Goes to the Doctor.* Adapted and illustrated by Lisa McCue. New York: Viking 1987.

Freeman, Lydia, *Corduroy's Toys.* New York: Viking, 1985.

Gag, Wanda, *Millions of Cats.* New York: Coward, McCann, 1977.

Gibbons, Gail:
*Check It Out.* San Diego: Harcourt Brace Jovanovich, 1985.
*Fill It Up.* New York: Harper & Row, 1985.
*The Milk Makers.* New York: Macmillan, 1985.

Greenaway, Kate, *Under the Window.* London: Frederick Warne & Co., 1879.

Gundersheimer, Karen:
*Colors to Know.* New York: Harper & Row, 1986.
*Shapes to Show.* New York: Harper & Row, 1986.

Hill, Eric:
*Spot Goes to the Circus.* New York: Putnam, 1986.
*Spot Goes to School.* New York: Putnam, 1984.
*Spot's First Walk.* New York: Putnam, 1981.
*Where's Spot?* New York: Putnam, 1980.

Hoban, Tana:
*Is It Larger? Is It Smaller?* New York: Greenwillow, 1985.
*Is It Red, Is It Yellow, Is It Blue?* New York: Greenwillow, 1978.
*Look Again.* New York: Macmillan, 1971.
*Panda Panda.* New York: Greenwillow, 1986.
*Red, Blue, Yellow Shoe.* New York: Greenwillow, 1986.

Hopkins, Lee Bennett, *Dinosaurs.* San Diego: Harcourt Brace Jovanovich, 1987.

Hutchins, Pat, *Rosie's Walk.* New York: Aladdin, 1971.

Jonas, Ann:
*Now We Can Go.* New York: Greenwillow, 1986.
*Where Can It Be?* New York: Greenwillow, 1986.

Keats, Ezra Jack, *The Snowy Day.* New York: Viking Penguin, 1964.

Krauss, Ruth. *The Carrot Seed.* Illustrated by Crockett Johnson. New York: Harper & Row, 1945.

Kunhardt, Dorothy, *Pat the Bunny.* Racine, Wisconsin: Western, 1942.

Larrick, Nancy, *When the Dark Comes Dancing: A Bedtime Poetry Book.* Illustrated by John Wallner. New York: Philomel Books, 1983.

MacDonald, Suse, *Alphabatics.* New York: Bradbury Press, 1986.

Maris, Ron:
*Are You There, Bear?* Greenwillow, 1984.
*Is Anyone Home?* Greenwillow, 1986.
*My Book.* Penguin, 1986.

Martin, Bill, Jr., *Brown Bear, Brown Bear. What Do You See?* New York: Holt, Rinehart & Winston, 1983.

Matthiesen, Thomas, *ABC: An Alphabet Book.* New York: Platt, 1966.

McCloskey, Robert, *Make Way for Ducklings!* New York: Viking Penguin, 1968.

Merriam, Eve, *Finding a Poem.* New York: Atheneum, 1970.

Milne, A. A., *Winnie the Pooh.* Illustrated by Ernest Shepard. New York: Dutton, 1961.

Oakley, Graham, *The Church Mice and the Moon.* New York: Macmillan 1974.

Ormerod, Jan.:
*Moonlight.* New York: Lothrop, Lee & Shepard Books, 1982.
*Sunshine.* New York: Lothrop, Lee & Shepard Books, 1981.

Oxenbury, Helen:

*Beach Day.* New York: Dial Books, 1982.
*Dressing.* New York: Simon and Schuster, 1981.
*Family.* New York: Simon and Schuster, 1981.
*Good Night, Good Morning.* New York: Dial Books, 1982.
*Mother's Helper.* New York: Dial Books, 1983.
*Shopping Trip.* New York: Dial Books, 1982.

Potter, Beatrix:
*Peter Rabbit's ABC.* New York: Warne (Viking), 1987.
*The Tale of Peter Rabbit.* London: Frederick Warne & Co. Inc., 1902.

Rackham, Arthur (Illus.), *Mother Goose: The Old Nursery Rhymes.* New York: Watts, 1969.

Rockwell, Anne, and Harlow Rockwell (illus.):
*Supermarket.* New York: Macmillan, 1979.
*The Toolbox.* New York: Macmillan, 1971.

Rockwell, Harlow:
*My Dentist,* New York: Greenwillow, 1975.
*My Doctor.* New York: Macmillan, 1973.

Saint-Saëns, Camille, and Noel Coward, *The Carnival of the Animals.* Recording and Poetry. Beverly Hills: Monitor, 1957.

Sendak, Maurice, *Where the Wild Things Are.* New York: Harper & Row, 1963.

Slobodkina, Esphyr, *Caps for Sale.* New York: Scholastic, 1984.

Stevenson, James, *Grandpa's Great City Tour.* New

York, Greenwillow, 1983.

Tafuri, Nancy, *Have You Seen My Duckling?* New York: Greenwillow, 1984.

Viorst, Judith, *The Tenth Good Thing about Barney.* New York: Atheneum, 1971.

Watson, Clyde and Wendy, *Catch Me, and Kiss Me, and Say It Again.* New York: Putnam, 1983.

Wells, Rosemary:
*Max's Bath.* New York: Dial, 1985.
*Max's Bedtime.* New York: Dial, 1985.
*Max's Birthday.* New York: Dial, 1985.
*Max's Breakfast.* New York: Dial, 1985.
*Max's First Word.* New York: Dial, 1979.
*Max's New Suit.* New York: Dial, 1979.
*Max's Ride.* New York: Dial, 1979.
*Max's Toys.* New York: Dial, 1979.

Wildsmith, Brian, *Brian Wildsmith's Mother Goose.* New York: Watts, 1965.

Wright, Blanche Fisher (illus.), *The Real Mother Goose.* New York: Macmillan, 1985.

Ziefert, Harriet, and illustrated by Arnold Lobel:
*Bear All Year.* New York: Harper & Row, 1986.
*Bear's Busy Morning.* New York: Harper & Row, 1986.
*Bear Gets Dressed.* New York: Harper & Row, 1986.
*Bear Goes Shopping.* New York: Harper & Row, 1986.

# Acknowledgments and Picture Credits

The index for this book was prepared by Louise Hedberg. The editors also thank: Alan Farstrup, International Reading Assoc., Newark, Del.; Penny Fiske, Fairfax County Public Library, Fairfax, Va.; Jerome Harste, Indiana University, Bloomington, Ind.; Julie Lando, Alexandria City Public Schools, Alexandria, Va.; Melvin D. Levine, M.D.; Karen Mitsoff, Alexandria, Va.; Sharon L. Murray, Children's Hospital National Medical Center, Washington D.C.; Joanne R. Nurss, Georgia State University, Atlanta, Ga.; Jean Osborn, University of Illinois, Champaign, Ill.

*The sources for the photographs in this book are listed below, followed by the sources for the illustrations. Credits from left to right are separated by semicolons; credits from top to bottom are separated by dashes.*

Photographs. Cover: Roger Foley. 7: Roger Foley. 8-15: Nancy Blackwelder. 32-35: Roger Foley. 37: Nancy Blackwelder. 43: Beecie Kupersmith. 51: Quesada/Burke Photography, courtesy *Scientific American*. 57: Roger Foley. 71: Nancy Blackwelder. 91: Roger Foley. 96: Tom Tracy. 119: Nancy Blackwelder.

Illustrations. 10-25: Marguerite E. Bell from photos by Beecie Kupersmith. 27: Cynthia Richardson. 38-44: Donald Gates from photos by Beecie Kupersmith. 46-47: Courtesy Judith A. Schickedanz. 49: From "Comprehension as Setting" in *New Perspectives on Comprehension* (Monograph in Language and Reading Studies) by J. C. Harste and R. F. Carey. Bloomington, Indiana: Language Education, Indiana University, 1979. 50-54: Courtesy Judith A. Schickedanz. 55: Courtesy Alexandra Marshall. 59: Jack Pardue from photo by Jane Jordan. 61-67: Jack Pardue from photos by Beecie Kupersmith. 68: Jack Pardue from photo by Jane Jordan. 72-73: Marguerite E. Bell from photos by Beecie Kupersmith, courtesy the Fairfax County Public Library, Fairfax, Virginia. 74: Jack Pardue from photo by Beecie Kupersmith. 78-79: John Drummond. 80-89: Jack Pardue from photos by Beecie Kupersmith. 93-99: Donald Gates from photos by Beecie Kupersmith. 100: John Drummond. 101: Donald Gates from photo by Jane Jordan. 103: John Drummond. 104: Donald Gates from photo by Beecie Kupersmith. 105: John Drummond. 107: Illustration by Clement Hurd in *Goodnight Moon* by Margaret Wise Brown. Copyright 1947, by Harper & Row, Publishers, Inc. Illustration copyright renewed © 1975 by Clement Hurd. Reprinted by permission of Harper & Row, Publishers, Inc. 108: From *The Tale of Peter Rabbit* by Beatrix Potter (Frederick Warne & Co., 1902), copyright © Frederick Warne & Co., 1902; from *Peter Pan in Kensington Garden* by J. M. Barrie, illustrated by Arthur Rackham, 1907, by permission of Barbara Edwards, courtesy of Charles Scribner's Sons — from *Hey Diddle Diddle* by Ralph Caldecott, 1882, courtesy of Frederick Warne & Co. All illustrations copied by Robert A. Grove, courtesy of the Illustrators' Collection, the D.C. Public Library, Washington, D.C. 109: From *Baby's Own Aesop: Being the Fable Condensed in Rhyme with Portable Morals Pictorially Printed* by Walter Crane, 1887, courtesy of Frederick Warne & Co. — from *Under the Window* by Kate Greenaway, 1879, courtesy of Frederick Warne & Co.; from *Winnie the Pooh* by A. A. Milne, illustrated by Ernest H. Shepard, copyright under the Berne Convention. Copyright 1926 by E. P. Dutton, renewed 1954 by A. A. Milne. Reproduced by permission of the publisher, E. P. Dutton, a division of NAL Penguin Inc. and Curtis Brown Ltd., London. All illustrations copied by Robert A. Grove, courtesy of the Illustrators' Collection, the D.C. Public Library, Washington, D.C. 110: From *Strega Nona* by Tomie de Paola © 1975. Used by permission of the publisher, Prentice-Hall, Inc., Englewood Cliffs, N.J., Tomie de Paola and the Kerlan Collection at the University of Minnesota; from *The Very Hungry Caterpillar* by Eric Carle. Copyright © 1969 by Eric Carle. Reproduced by permission of Philomel Books — from *Make Way for Ducklings* by Robert McCloskey. Copyright 1941, renewed © 1968 by Robert McCloskey. Reproduced by permission of Viking Penguin Inc. — from *Freight Train* written and illustrated by Donald Crews. Copyright © 1978 by Donald Crews. Reproduced by permission of Greenwillow Books (A Division of William Morrow & Co.). 111: From *Whistle for Willie* by Ezra Jack Keats. Copyright © 1964 by Ezra Jack Keats. Reproduced by permission of Viking Penguin Inc. — from *Where the Wild Things Are* by Maurice Sendak. Copyright © 1963 by Maurice Sendak. Reprinted by permission of Harper & Row, Publishers, Inc.; from *Madeline* by Ludwig Bemelmans. Copyright 1939 by Ludwig Bemelmans. Copyright renewed © 1966 by Madeleine Bemelmans and Barbara Bemelmans Marciano. Reproduced by permission of Viking Penguin Inc. 113: Donald Gates from photo by Beecie Kupersmith. 115-117: William Hennessy, Jr. from photos by Beecie Kupersmith. Projects created by Beecie Kupersmith and Anne Muñoz-Furlong. 121: Kathe Scherr from photo by Beecie Kupersmith. 123: From *Here We Are* by Richard L. Allington, et al. Scott, Foresman Reading: An American Tradition. Copyright © 1987 by Scott, Foresman and Company. Reprinted by permission. 125: John Drummond. 128: From *Phonics Workbook, Level A* published by Modern Curriculum Press, Cleveland, Ohio. Copyright © 1988 by Modern Curriculum Press, Inc. Reprinted by permission. 129: From *Friends* by Richard L. Allington, et al. Scott, Foresman Reading: an American Tradition. Copyright © 1987 by Scott, Foresman and Company. Reprinted by permission. 132: Kathe Scherr from photo by Beecie Kupersmith. 134-137: Marguerite E. Bell from photos by Beecie Kupersmith, courtesy of the Maury School, Alexandria, Va.

# Index

Time-Life Books Inc. offers a wide range of fine recordings, including a *Rock 'n' Roll Era* series. For subscription information, call 1-800-621-7026, or write TIME-LIFE MUSIC, P.O. Box C-32068, Richmond, Virginia 23261-2068